Performance Optimization of Digital Communications Systems

OTHER TELECOMMUNICATIONS BOOKS FROM AUERBACH

**Chaos Applications in
Telecommunications**
Peter Stavroulakis
ISBN: 0-8493-3832-8

Fundamentals of DSL Technology
Philip Golden; Herve Dedieu; Krista S Jacobsen
ISBN: 0-8493-1913-7

**IP Multimedia Subsystem: Service
Infrastructure to Converge NGN,
3G and the Internet**
Rebecca Copeland
ISBN: 0-8493-9250-0

Mobile Middleware
Paolo Bellavista and Antonio Corradi
ISBN: 0-8493-3833-6

MPLS for Metropolitan Area Networks
Nam-Kee Tan
ISBN: 0-8493-2212-X

**Network Security Technologies,
Second Edition**
Kwok T Fung
ISBN: 0-8493-3027-0

**Performance Modeling and Analysis of
Bluetooth Networks: Polling, Scheduling,
and Traffic Control**
Jelena Misic and Vojislav B Misic
ISBN: 0-8493-3157-9

**Performance Optimization of Digital
Communications Systems**
Vladimir Mitlin
ISBN: 0-8493-6896-0

**A Practical Guide to Content Delivery
Networks**
Gilbert Held
ISBN: 0-8493-3649-X

**Resource, Mobility and Security
Management in Wireless Networks
and Mobile Communications**
Yan Zhang, Honglin Hu, and Masayuki Fujise
ISBN: 0-8493-8036-7

**Service-Oriented Architectures
in Telecommunications**
Vijay K Gurbani; Xian-He Sun
ISBN: 0-8493-9567-4

**Testing Integrated QoS of VoIP: Packets
to Perceptual Voice Quality**
Vlatko Lipovac
ISBN: 0-8493-3521-3

**Traffic Management in IP-Based
Communications**
Trinh Anh Tuan
ISBN: 0-8493-9577-1

**Understanding Broadband over
Power Line**
Gilbert Held
ISBN: 0-8493-9846-0

**WiMAX: A Wireless Technology
Revolution**
G.S.V. Radha Krishna Rao; G. Radhamani
ISBN: 0-8493-7059-0

WiMAX: Taking Wireless to the MAX
Deepak Pareek
ISBN: 0-8493-7186-4

Wireless Mesh Networks
Gilbert Held
ISBN: 0-8493-2960-4

Wireless Security Handbook
Aaron E Earle
ISBN: 0-8493-3378-4

Performance Optimization of Digital Communications Systems

Vladimir Mitlin

CRC Press
Taylor & Francis Group
Boca Raton London New York

CRC Press is an imprint of the
Taylor & Francis Group, an **informa** business

AN AUERBACH BOOK

First published 2006 by Auerbach Publications

Published 2019 by CRC Press
Taylor & Francis Group
6000 Broken Sound Parkway NW, Suite 300
Boca Raton, FL 33487-2742

© 2006 by Taylor & Francis Group
CRC Press is an imprint of Taylor & Francis Group, an Informa business

First issued in paperback 2019

No claim to original U.S. Government works

ISBN-13: 978-0-367-45377-0 (pbk)
ISBN-13: 978-0-8493-6896-7 (hbk)

**Visit the Taylor & Francis Web site at
http://www.taylorandfrancis.com**

**and the CRC Press Web site at
http://www.crcpress.com**

Library of Congress Cataloging-in-Publication Data

Mitlin, Vladimir S. (Vladimir Solomon), 1959-
    Performance optimization of digital communications systems / Vladimir Mitlin.
        p. cm.
    Includes bibliographical references and index.
    ISBN 0-8493-6896-0 (alk. paper)
    1. Digital communications. 2. Network performance (Telecommunica on) I. Title.

TK5103.7.M477 2006
621.382--dc22   2005057244

Library of Congress Card Number 2005057244

Author

Vlad Mitlin received an M.Sc. degree in applied mathematics from the Moscow Oil and Gas Institute, Moscow, Russia, in 1981 and a Ph.D. in fluid mechanics from the National Gas Research Institute, Moscow, Russia, in 1987.

During 1987 to 1990, he was a research associate with the Earth Physics Institute of the Russian Academy of Sciences. During 1990 to 1994, he was a postdoctoral fellow at the Engineering College of the University of Texas at Austin conducting research in statistical thermodynamics and nonlinear dynamics. During 1994 to 1995, he was a software consultant at Nielsen North America, Schaumburg, Illinois. From 1995 to 1997, he was a manager of fluid mechanics research at TerraTek, Salt Lake City, Utah. From 1997 to 1999, he was a senior software engineer at the Advanced/Functional Test Department of 3Com Corporation, Salt Lake City, Utah. From 1999 to 2002, he was a senior staff member at the Technology Development Center of 3Com Corporation, San Diego, California. From 2002 to 2003 he was chief scientist at the Metric Systems Corporation, Vista, California. Currently, he is an independent consultant.

He has published a book (*Nonlinear Dynamics of Reservoir Mixtures,* CRC Press, Boca Raton, 1993) and about 80 articles in professional publications. His research interests include digital communications, nonlinear dynamics, fluid mechanics of heterogeneous systems, and inverse problems.

Dedication

To Carole

Contents

Chapter 1

Introduction

1.1 About This Book

It is undoubtedly correct to say that digital communications, as a branch of engineering, is currently at an advanced stage. The market competition among similar products manufactured by different companies is fierce, and attaining even a small performance advantage for a particular product may drastically change a company's financial standing. What becomes especially important in these circumstances is the fine-tuning of parameters of modern digital communications systems, yielding optimized system performance.

This book is about the performance optimization of digital communications systems. I started working on this topic at the end of 1999 when I joined the Technology Development Center of 3Com in San Diego. The group I joined worked on advancing the Asymmetrical Digital Subscriber Line (ADSL) technology at that time, and I was assigned to research the problem of optimizing parameters of the physical and media access layers of ADSL. This activity turned out to involve analytical tools of applied mathematics to a high degree that I, an applied mathematician by training, particularly enjoyed. Now, I can say that, in this kind of activity, there should be a balance between analytical methods and simulations. Using analytical methods only leaves you vulnerable, because these methods always work under certain suppositions. There is no guarantee that everything is kosher with your math until some confirming simulations have been performed. On the other hand, not using analytical methods eliminates the most important abstraction layer in your research.

I realized in the beginning of 2005 that the different performance optimization topics I had worked on throughout the past years could be unified into this monograph that you are now reading. This monograph is structured such that each chapter describes a particular optimization problem in digital communications. Throughout the book, analytical techniques are presented in combination with SystemView and Matlab simulations.

This monograph consists of ten chapters; references are given after each chapter. I realize that the literature on digital communications is huge, and I extend apologies to researchers whose results have not been cited here.

Chapter 2 describes the problem of determining the quality of a communication channel; specifically, reliably estimating the signal-to-noise ratio (SNR) of the channel in a complex multipath propagation environment.

Chapter 3 introduces a method for proprietary data transmission. The essence of the method is transmitting a message over a communication channel using a "smart noise" whose stochastic properties are associated with this message.

Chapter 4 describes a method of pulse shaping or, more specifically, of generating low-complexity, spectrally efficient pulses for digital communications.

Chapter 5 describes a method of reducing the peak-to-average power ratio and introduces optimal phase shifters for multicarrier communication systems.

Chapter 6 presents a general methodology for optimal selection of the automatic repeat request (ARQ) parameters in quadrature amplitude modulation channels.

Chapter 7 presents a method of performance optimization of multicarrier systems with forward error correction and automatic repeat request.

In Chapter 8, the procedure of estimating the bit error rate of self-similar constellations in ADSL systems is discussed.

In Chapter 9, an exact solution is developed for the throughput of a general duplex communications channel with forward error correction and automatic repeat request.

Chapter 10 presents an analytical method of optimal breaking of a Transmission Control Protocol/Internet Protocol (TCP/IP) message into MAC packets in networks such as those compliant with the IEEE 802.11 wireless LAN standard.

To make this book more readable, I have included a lot of pictures. Also, if you get stressed at any moment while reading this book, there are some optimization puzzles in Appendix A for you to try. Appendix B contains a few MatLab scripts relevant to the project described in Chapter 4. Appendix C presents some newly discovered properties of flat-spectrum and spectrum-shaped waveforms.

1.2 Acknowledgments

A significant part of the results included in Chapter 6 to Chapter 10 was developed from 1999 to 2001, when I was with 3Com Corporation in San Diego. I am grateful to the company management for supporting this research.

Results in Chapter 7 and Chapter 9 are obtained in collaboration with Richard Williams [1,2]. I am grateful to Richard for the numerous discussions we have had on digital communications over the years. They were enlightening and gave me a deeper understanding of the digital communications theory. Likewise, some of the results presented in Chapter 6 are part of the patent [3].

Chapter 6: I am grateful to Joseph Mueller and Richard Williams for their useful comments. The discussions on automatic repeat request (ARQ) at the meetings of IEEE 802.16 standard committee that I attended in 2000 and 2001 were very stimulating.

Chapter 7: Joseph Mueller provided me with results of his numerical simulations of a G.992.2 ADSL channel.

Chapter 10: I am grateful to Tim Murphy, Paul Sherer, and Ilya Volvovsky for useful discussions.

Last but not least, special thanks to my wife Carole. She was a source of constant support and encouragement throughout this work. Moreover, as it was she who typed the entire manuscript, it is fair to say that she was literally the hands of this project.

Vlad Mitlin

References

1. Mitlin, V., Williams, R.G.C., Performance Evaluation of Multicarrier Channels with Forward Error Correction and Automatic Repeat Request, U.S. Patent Application No. 20020108081, pending.
2. Mitlin, V., Williams, R.G.C., Performance Evaluation of Multicarrier Channels, U.S. Patent Application No. 20030105997, pending.
3. Mitlin, V., Mueller, J., Method and Apparatus for Selection of ARQ Parameters and Estimation of Improved Communications, U.S. Patent No. 6,718,493, 2004.

Chapter 2

Method for Determining the Quality of a Communication Channel

2.1 Background

In digital communications, a precise knowledge of the parameters characterizing the quality of a communication channel is extremely important for efficient data transmission. The classical Shannon result states that the data rate of a communication channel is a function of the signal-to-noise ratio (SNR). For a given signal, the increase in the noise level adversely affects the quality of transmission. The amount of information that can be reliably transmitted over a communication channel decreases as the noise increases [1–3].

The precise knowledge of the SNR of a channel dictates how much information will ultimately be transmitted. If one underestimates the SNR, the channel efficiency drops compared to the most efficient transmission mode. If one overestimates the SNR, then more data is transmitted but the information is less reliable. Therefore, it is extremely important to be able to estimate the SNR of a communication channel in a precise and timely manner.

This is even more important in modern wireless communications that meet new challenges with respect to increasingly complex propagation environments. Typical examples of such environments would be urban areas, office buildings, military vessels, war zones, jungles, rock concerts, etc. Some of these environments are characterized by severe multipath effects, some by strong fading, and others by both. When a communication session between two stations is initiated in such an environment, the SNR should be measured on both ends of the channel as precisely as possible, and further communications over this channel must be stipulated by the SNR value measured [4–8].

This chapter describes the problem of determining the quality of a communication channel and, more particularly, how to reliably estimate the SNR of a channel in a complex multipath propagation environment [9]. We present methods for estimating the level of interferers in a spectral window of a given bandwidth of a communication channel. The first method of estimating the level of interferers comprises generating and transmitting a baseband signal consisting of several sine wave sets on the Nyquist frequency and with phases evenly spanning the interval $(0, 2\pi)$ radians. The second method of estimating the level of interferers comprises generating and transmitting several sine wave sequences of the same phase with frequencies evenly spanning a vicinity of the Nyquist frequency. There is an agreement established between the transmitting and receiving stations, determining the duration of time intervals between successive sine wave sequences. This duration should not be smaller than the maximum delay in the channel determined from a separate test.

2.2 Main Idea Illustrated and a Minimization Principle

The main idea of the method of determining the level of interferers in a spectral window of a given bandwidth presented in the following text is to generate a special baseband signal at the transmitting station. This signal may be one of two kinds. The first is a concatenation of several sine wave sequences with frequencies equal to the Nyquist frequency of the spectral window and phases evenly spanning the interval of $(0, 2\pi)$ radians. The second is a concatenation of several sine wave sequences of the same phase and frequencies evenly spanning a small vicinity of the Nyquist frequency of the spectral window. This idea is illustrated by a set of SystemView simulations of increasing complexity.

Figure 2.1 shows the simplest arrangement. The propagation environment is described by a multipath channel model with ten paths, a maximum delay value of 0.3 sec, and the value of the K-factor is 1.

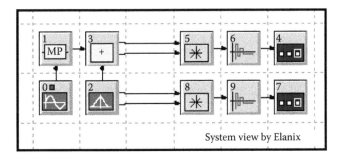

Figure 2.1   An illustrative system for estimating the level of interferers.

This severe environment is aggravated by the presence of additive white Gaussian noise (AWGN). Depending on the intricacy of the transmitter and receiver, the multipath distortion of a signal may or may not be a negative effect. Specifically, if the RAKE receiver is used, the information contained in indirect paths will be utilized and will actually improve the quality of the signal received. If the receiver does not have such capabilities, the multipath distortion presents a negative effect. Of course, the presence of AWGN is always a negative factor for transmission.

Consider a baseband channel sampled with the frequency of 128 Hz. The test for determining the noise level comprises transmitting several sine wave sequences of increasing frequency and phase of 0. Seven sequences are transmitted while the sine wave frequency changes by 1 Hz from 60 Hz to 67 Hz. Notice that our simulation describes spanning the spectrum in the vicinity of the Nyquist frequency, which in this particular case, is equal to 64 Hz. Figure 2.2 and Figure 2.3 present the results. Figure 2.2 corresponds to the actual AWGN variance of 10^{-14} V^2 and Figure 2.3 to 1 V^2. All three figures show both an actual and estimated noise variance versus the sine wave frequency. The value of the AWGN variance at the Nyquist frequency measured at the receiver is exactly equal to the actual value. It is especially stunning how different the variance values estimated at the Nyquist and non-Nyquist frequencies are. For example, in Figure 2.2, the difference is about 14 orders.

2.3 Phase-Spanning Nyquist Set Test

The simulation described is somewhat idealistic. It assumes that one can perfectly synchronize the transmitter and receiver such that there would be no phase shift between the transmitted and the received

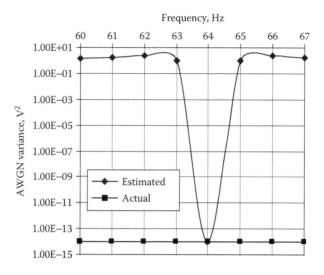

Figure 2.2 A set of actual and estimated noise variances obtained at frequencies of 60 Hz, 61 Hz, 62 Hz, 63 Hz, 64 Hz, 65 Hz, 66 Hz, and 67 Hz by using the system shown in Figure 2.1.

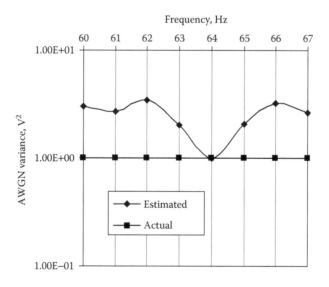

Figure 2.3 A set of actual and estimated noise variances obtained at frequencies of 60 Hz, 61 Hz, 62 Hz, 63 Hz, 64 Hz, 65 Hz, 66 Hz, and 67 Hz by using the system shown in Figure 2.1.

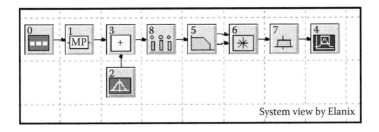

Figure 2.4   A baseband system for estimating the level of interferers.

signals. In reality, such a phase shift is very hard to control. Therefore, the following generalization of the method is proposed. The test comprises transmitting several sine wave sequences on the Nyquist frequency. Each sequence is characterized by a certain phase value. The set of phase values is arranged so that it evenly spans the interval $(0, 2\pi)$. There is an agreement established between the transmitting station and the receiving station determining the duration of time intervals between successive sine wave sequences. This duration should exceed the maximum delay in the channel, determined from a separate test preceding the SNR measurement. For each sequence, one determines an average square of the magnitude of the received signal. The minimum value of this parameter over all datasets yields an estimate of the level of interferers. Determining the level of interferers, as described above, can be attained by means of transmitting a single wave form termed the *phase-spanning Nyquist* (PSN) set.

Figure 2.4 shows the next system considered. This is a continuous system for SNR estimation. Token 0 represents a PSN set generator described by the following equation:

$$s(t) = A \sin\left(\pi ft + \left(\frac{2\pi n}{N}\right)\left\lfloor \frac{ft}{n} \right\rfloor\right) \qquad (2.3.1)$$

In this equation, s(t) is the signal transmitted, f is the sampling rate (or, equivalently, the two-sided bandwidth of the spectral window where the SNR is to be determined), N is the total number of samples in the test, n is a parameter for determining the number of samples used in the averager (token 7), A is the signal amplitude chosen from the condition of equality of values of an average transmitted power of a PSN set (i.e., half the A value squared) and of a signal used in actual data transmission, and $\lfloor x \rfloor$ denotes the maximum integer not

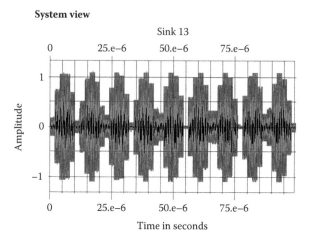

Figure 2.5   An example of a phase-spanning Nyquist (PSN) set.

exceeding a given real number x. This signal is transmitted over the channel and is down-converted, sampled, and filtered on the receiver. Then it is squared and averaged (token 7) with a window of $nD{-}r$ seconds, where $D = (1/f)$ is a spacing between samples, and r is the maximum delay in the channel, determined in a separate test. The result goes into a sink (token 9) in which the minimum of the average variance over all sequences is determined. This yields an estimate of the level of interferers.

Parameters for this simulator are as follows: sampling rate = 128E+6 Hz; n = 256, a channel with one path, the maximum delay of 200E–9 sec, and the K-factor of 1; total number of samples in a PSN set is N = 64n, the amplitude of the PSN set is 1 V; the sampling jitter constant equals $D/10$. The low-pass filter applied at the receiver is the Butterworth filter with ten poles and a cutoff frequency of 62E+6 Hz.

Figure 2.5 presents the PSN set transmitted in this test. The PSN set is nearly (but not exactly) periodical with the period of about $1/9$ of the test duration.

Figure 2.6 presents SNR test results for several different levels of AWGN. The estimated values agree with the actual ones. Note that more precision is lost as the level of noise decreases.

Figure 2.7 presents the results of an SNR test in which two types of interferers affect the channel, e.g., AWGN and PN sequence with the rate of 12.8E+6 Hz. The magnitude of the PN sequence is chosen to be equal to the mean square deviation of AWGN. The estimated and the actual data are in excellent agreement. We did not observe

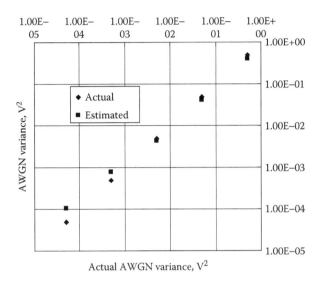

Figure 2.6 An estimated versus the actual level of interferers obtained by using PSN sets in the system shown in Figure 2.4.

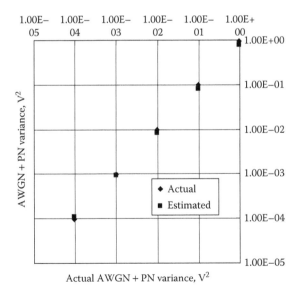

Figure 2.7 An estimated versus the actual level of interferers obtained by using PSN sets in the system shown in Figure 2.4.

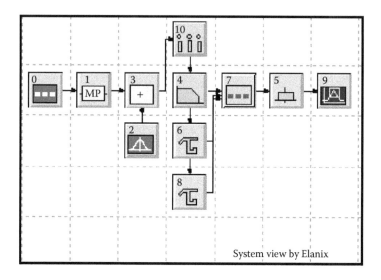

System view by Elanix

Figure 2.8 A baseband system for estimating the level of interferers.

any performance deterioration of the SNR estimator at lower noise levels. This is probably due to the mutual compensation of errors caused by noises from two sources.

We are able to achieve an even better performance of an SNR estimator, especially in the range of high SNR. The corresponding system is shown in Figure 2.8. The wave form transmitted is a PSN set (token 0). The precision of the estimation is improved due to the use of a more sophisticated estimator involving current and delayed samples instead of just squaring the current signal value. This operation is implemented by token 7 in Figure 2.8. The inputs to this token are the current signal value and the ones delayed by one and two samples, respectively (token 6 and token 8). Token 7 performs the following calculation:

$$\text{Output} = s(t) \times (s(t) + 2 \times s(t - D) + s(t - 2 \times D)) \quad (2.3.2)$$

The estimator, using Equation 2.3.1 and Equation 2.3.2, has the precision of about 1 dB in the entire range of noise measurements taken.

It was observed that at high SNR, the time dependence of the noise variance usually has a distinctive global minimum. On the contrary, at low SNR, this dependence typically has several local minima with values close to that of the global minimum. To determine the global minimum in this case, this time series should go through an additional data processing routine at low SNR. First, this dependence is raised to a power of m; we found that m = 32 works well. The next step is integrating the result of this transformation over time. The final step is to divide the result of integration by the total test time and to raise the result to a power of $1/m$. This data treatment improves the estimation results at low SNR and leaves them nearly unchanged at high SNR.

2.4 Frequency-Spanning Nyquist Set Test

This section introduces another method of determining the level of interferers with a wave form termed *frequency-spanning Nyquist* (FSN) set. The basic idea is not to generate sine waves on a Nyquist frequency while spanning the entire phase range evenly but rather to span the frequency range in a small vicinity of the Nyquist frequency. Depending on the characteristics of the transmitter, the use of either FSN or PSN set may be preferred.

The system considered in the following text is equivalent to the one shown in Figure 2.4 except that token 0 now generates the following wave form:

$$s(t) = A \sin\left[\pi \, ft\left(1 - b + \left(\frac{2nb}{N}\right)\left\lfloor\frac{ft}{n}\right\rfloor\right)\right] \qquad (2.4.1)$$

In Equation 2.4.1, s(t) is the signal transmitted; f is the sampling frequency; N is the total number of samples in an FSN set; b is the parameter used in determining the size of the vicinity of the Nyquist frequency in the spectrum spanned in the test, i.e.,

$$\left(\frac{f(1-b)}{2}, \frac{f(1+b)}{2}\right);$$

n defines the window in the averager in Figure 2.4 as nD–r; and A is the FSN set amplitude determined from the condition of equality of values of an average transmitted power of an FSN set and a signal used in actual data transmission.

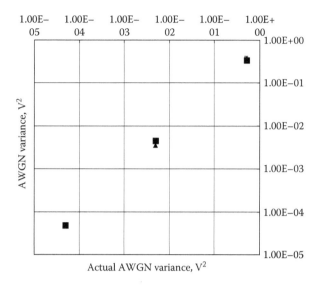

Figure 2.9   An estimated versus the actual level of interferers obtained by using FSN sets in the system shown in Figure 2.4.

Figure 2.9 to Figure 2.10 present simulation results of an FSN set test. Simulation parameters are sampling rate = 128 MHz; N = 16,384; n = 256; sampler aperture and aperture jitter are both equal to $D/4$; a multipath channel with one path, r = 200E–9 sec, and K-factor = 1; b = 0.01; and A = 1 V. To obtain each data point, the test was run three times as shown in the figures. Figure 2.9 presents results in the case of the AWGN only; Figure 2.10 corresponds to a channel distortion by two interferers, AWGN, and a harmonic wave with the frequency of 12.8E+6 Hz. In the last case, the amplitude of each periodical interferer was set to be equal to the mean square deviation of AWGN. The results show a good agreement between actual and estimated levels of interferers (e.g., the maximum deviation of an estimate from the actual value was never larger than 1 dB).

2.5 Determining the Noise Level in a Nonbaseband System

This section gives the most important proof of the concept presented in this chapter. Specifically, we describe the results of simulating the SNR test including up- or down-conversion of the baseband signal. Figure 2.11 presents the system considered. Token 0 implements a

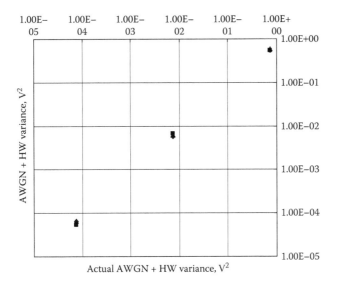

Figure 2.10   An estimated versus the actual level of interferers obtained by using FSN sets in the system shown in Figure 2.4.

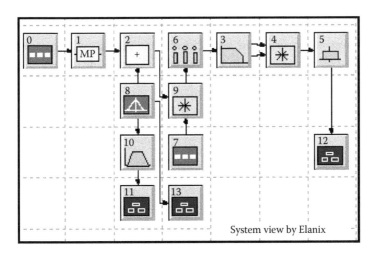

Figure 2.11   A nonbaseband system for estimating the level of interferers.

signal generator. In the case of a PSN set, it generates the following signal:

$$s(t) = A \sin\left(2\pi ht + \pi ft + \left(\frac{2\pi n}{N}\right)\left\lfloor\frac{ft}{n}\right\rfloor\right) \qquad (2.5.1)$$

In Equation 2.5.1, we use the same notations as in Equation 2.3.1, with one new parameter, h, representing the carrier frequency. In the case of an FSN set, the following signal is generated:

$$s(t) = A \sin\left(2\pi ht + \pi ft\left(1 - b + \left(\frac{2bn}{N}\right)\left\lfloor\frac{ft}{n}\right\rfloor \right) \right) \quad (2.5.2)$$

The signal is then transmitted over a multipath channel (token 1), and it is also corrupted by an additive noise (token 8). In the receiver, the signal is down-converted by multiplying it by:

$$s(t) = \sin\left(2\pi ht + F \right) \quad (2.5.3)$$

(token 7); F is a phase shift between signals at the transmitting and receiving stations. Then the signal is sampled (token 6), filtered (token 3), squared (token 4), and averaged (token 5) with a window whose parameters were discussed in earlier sections. The results are collected over the test duration and the minimum is determined, which yields an estimate of the noise level (token 12).

The parameters used in simulations are as follows: the carrier is a harmonic wave with an amplitude of 1 V and frequency of 256E+6 Hz. The carrier is sampled at a rate of 1024E+6 Hz. The baseband signal is sampled at a rate of 128E+6 Hz. Then the Butterworth low-pass filter with ten poles and a cutoff frequency of 62E+6 Hz is applied. This means that the spectral window scanned is 194E+6 Hz to 318E+6 Hz. The actual level of noise in this window is determined by passing the noise through a band pass filter (token 10). In this set of simulations, the aperture and jitter of the sampler presented by token 6 on the receiver are both 0.

Figure 2.12 shows the Fourier spectrum of the noise at the outlet of token 10. Figure 2.13 to Figure 2.19 present the results of the SNR test with AWGN as the only interferer. Note that the variance of the transmitted signal is 0.5 V².

Figure 2.13 presents the results of the SNR test using a PSN set; the total number of samples is 16,384 (i.e., the total number of baseband samples is 2048). In the low- and intermediate-SNR range, the typical variation of results is negligible, whereas the variation is considerable in high-SNR range. Figure 2.14 shows the results with the same parameters except that the total number of samples is 65,536 (or

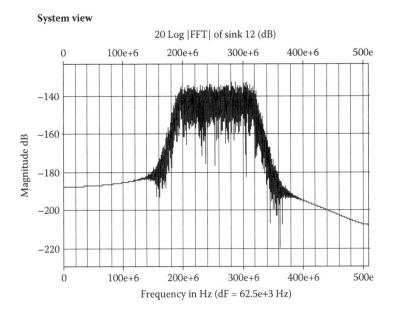

Figure 2.12   The noise spectrum in the spectral window scanned.

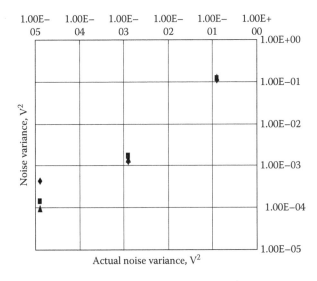

Figure 2.13   An estimated versus the actual level of interferers obtained by using PSN sets in the system shown in Figure 2.11.

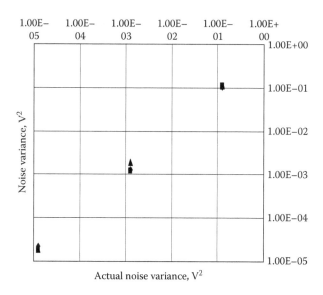

Figure 2.14 An estimated versus the actual level of interferers obtained by using PSN sets in the system shown in Figure 2.11.

total number of baseband samples is 8192). Increasing the number of samples makes the variation in the results in the high-SNR range also negligible. Figure 2.15 presents the results with the same set of parameters that was used in generating Figure 2.13 except for the sampler parameters; at the receiving station, after down-conversion, the PSN set is sampled with the aperture of 1.95E–9 sec and the jitter constant of 0.97E–9 sec. The results show a consistent underestimation of the noise variance by about 3 dB in the entire SNR range studied.

Figure 2.16 presents the results of an SNR test using an FSN set with b = 0.01, the total number of samples = 16,384, and the signal was assumed to be sampled at the receiving station without jitter. Figure 2.17 shows the results with the same parameters except that the total number of samples was 65,536. Again, an increase in the total number of samples in the wave form used for this test improves the precision of the estimated level of noise in the high-SNR range. Figure 2.18 presents the results with the same set of parameters that was used in generating Figure 2.16 except for the sampler parameters; at the receiving station, after down-conversion, the FSN set is sampled with the aperture of 1.95E-9 sec and the jitter constant of 0.97E–9 sec. The results show a consistent underestimation of the noise variance by about 3 dB in the entire SNR range studied.

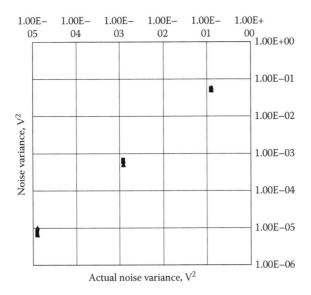

Figure 2.15 An estimated versus the actual level of interferers obtained by using PSN sets in the system shown in Figure 2.11.

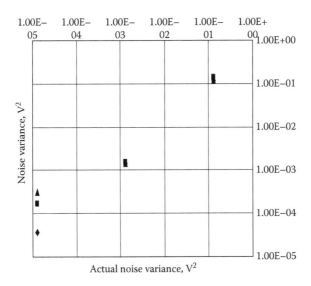

Figure 2.16 An estimated versus the actual level of interferers obtained by using FSN sets in the system shown in Figure 2.11.

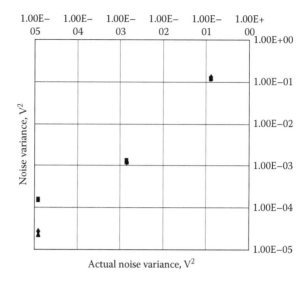

Figure 2.17 **An estimated versus the actual level of interferers obtained by using FSN sets in the system shown in Figure 2.11.**

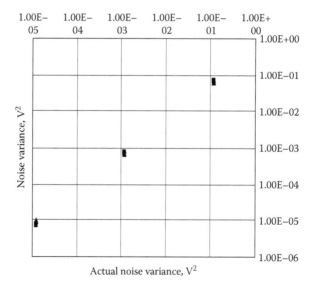

Figure 2.18 **An estimated versus the actual level of interferers obtained by using FSN sets in the system shown in Figure 2.11.**

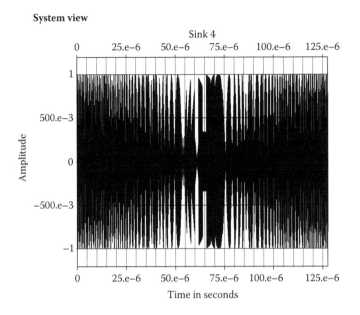

Figure 2.19   An example of a frequency-spanning Nyquist (FSN) set.

Figure 2.19 presents an example of an FSN set generated at the transmitting station. Also, we have run simulations for the same set of parameters but varying the phase shift F. This is important to determine how large the variation in the results would be if the signal detection were performed noncoherently and F were not controlled. In all cases, the effect of choosing F at random did not exceed 0.5 dB.

2.6 Measuring the Level of a Useful Signal

So far, we concentrated on determining the level of interferers in the channel. One also has to determine the level of a useful signal at the receiving station. This is accomplished by transmitting several repetitions of the signal.

Simulations were performed to determine how many repetitions of a signal one has to transmit to be able to reliably determine its level. Initial data is a sampling rate of 128 MHz; a channel with one path, a maximum delay of 200E-9 sec, and a K-factor of 1; AWGN with mean square deviation of 0.71 V; and a sampling jitter of D/10. The signal used was a chirp with an amplitude of 1 V, a start frequency of 0 Hz, a stop frequency of 25 MHz, and a period of 1E-6 sec. Our results show that an estimated level of the chirp converges to its true value as the number of repetitions is about 32.

2.7 Conclusions

This chapter introduces a method for estimating the level of interferers and the level of a useful signal in a communication channel in a complex multipath propagation environment. The method uses a special waveform that can be either the PSN set (Equation 2.3.1) or the FSN set (Equation 2.4.1). The method comprises:

Determining the maximum delay in the channel by sending a pulse from the transmitting station to the receiving station

Generating either a PSN set (Equation 2.3.1) or an FSN set (Equation 2.4.1) at the transmitting station

Up-converting this signal and transmitting it from the transmitting station

At the receiving station, down-converting the signal, sampling it, and passing it through a filter

At the receiving station, squaring the signal or, in the case of a PSN set, applying the transformation given by Equation 2.3.2

At the receiving station, averaging the result with a window smaller than the parameter n in Equation 2.3.1 or Equation 2.4.1 by the maximum delay in the channel determined earlier

At the receiving station, determining the minimum of the result over the duration of the test, which determines the level of noise in the channel

At the transmitting station, sending several repetitions of the signal used for actual data transmission

At the receiving station, down-converting, sampling, and filtering the signal

At the receiving station, squaring and averaging the result that determines the level of a useful signal plus the level of noise

At the receiving station, determining the level of a useful signal and, by applying the level of noise value, calculating the channel SNR

In this chapter, we presented a method of determining the channel quality between two stations. Our method also describes a procedure for determining the quality of data transmission in a network if these two stations are nodes of the network.

The essence of this method of estimating the level of interferers in a spectral window of a given bandwidth is generating and transmitting several sets of sine waves <u>on or around the Nyquist frequency for this window</u>. This is what makes this method work even for very complex propagation environments and determines its performance characteristics.

References

1. Proakis, J.G., *Digital Communications*, McGraw-Hill, New York, 1995.
2. Proakis, J.G., Salehi, M., *Contemporary Communication Systems Using Matlab*, Brooks/Cole, Pacific Grove, 2000.
3. Bertsekas, D., Gallager, R., *Data Networks*, Prentice-Hall, NJ, 1992.
4. Urbanski, S.A., Energy Estimator and Method Therefore, U.S. Patent No. 5,666,429, 1997.
5. Lindbom, L., Jamal, K., Low Complexity Model Based Channel Estimation Algorithm for Fading Channels, U.S. Patent No. 5,581,580, 1996.
6. Fleming-Dahl, A., Average Signal to Noise Ratio Estimator, U.S. Patent No. 6,442,495, 2002.
7. Schiff, L.N., Method and Apparatus for Operating an Adaptive Decision Feedback Equalizer, U.S. Patent No. 6,298,242, 2001.
8. Cai, L., System and Method for Bit Loading with Optimal Margin Assignment, U.S. Patent No. 6,205,410, 2001.
9. Mitlin, V., Method for Determining the Quality of a Communication Channel, U.S. Patent Application No. 10/729,740.

Chapter 3

Digital Communications in Stealth Mode

3.1 Background

Methods of transmitting proprietary data are in demand for both civil and military applications. Transmitting proprietary data is a challenging problem for the following reasons: On the one hand, if the proprietary data were intercepted, it should not be easily deciphered by an enemy (in military applications) or by a competitor (in business applications). On the other hand, proprietary data should be successfully deciphered by their intended recipient.

A traditional approach to transmitting proprietary data consists of encoding a given proprietary message in a nonrandom signal and then hiding that signal in a noise-like background. However, because the signal used for encoding is not random, it will be retrieved by an enemy or a competitor as soon as they are able to recognize the presence of a useful signal in the noisy background and separate this signal from the noise. It would be very useful to introduce a proprietary data transmission technique that is free of this drawback.

The main idea of the stealth communication method described in the following text is not to hide a nonrandom information-bearing signal in a noisy background but rather to use a special kind of an information-bearing noise. This "smart" noise is indistinguishable by its spectral properties from the noise in the communication channel, yet it has an internal structure that allows the intended recipient to successfully retrieve the proprietary message encoded in the noise. Moreover, such a smart noise (SN) can be combined with a decoy signal, the latter having a regular nonrandom structure and may be of a larger power than the SN. In this case, an enemy or a competitor will be misled and will try to retrieve whatever information is encoded in the decoy signal. It will be shown that it is possible to design the structure of the SN in such a way that combining it with a much stronger decoy signal does not distort this structure and even enhances the retrieval properties of the SN.

3.2 Stealth Communications Transceiver

Figure 3.1 presents an outline of the stealth communication system, illustrating the concept described earlier. The system consists of a transmitter, channel, and receiver. Transmission over a baseband *additive white Gaussian noise* (AWGN) channel sampled with the rate of 128 Hz was simulated in SystemView.

The transmitter is represented by tokens 0, 1, 2, 9, 15, and 21. Token 9 represents a source of raw random data. In this case, it generates a PN sequence of the amplitude of 1 V at the rate of 128 Hz. The output of this token may be either +1 or −1. Generally, a subsystem represented by token 9 should generate a time series with statistical and spectral properties that are similar to those of the noise in the communication channel. This requirement is easy to satisfy if the channel noise can be represented by the noise sampled locally at the transmitter. Otherwise, one must be able to estimate some of the parameters of the channel noise at the receiver. The corresponding methods have been published [1]. In the case of limited information about the channel, the minimum requirement of the time series is that its magnitude should be approximately on or below the level of the channel noise.

The time series generated by token 9 is separated into two random data streams. The first (token 0) is generated as follows:

$$\text{output} = \frac{(\text{current input} + \text{input delayed by one sample})}{2} \quad (3.2.1)$$

The second (token 1) is generated as follows:

$$\text{output} = \frac{(\text{current input} - \text{input delayed by one sample})}{2} \quad (3.2.2)$$

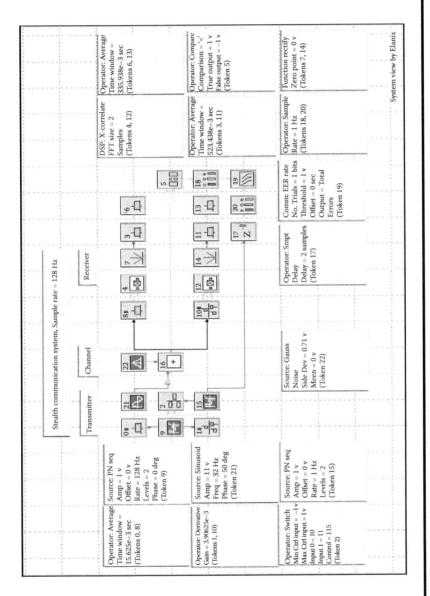

Figure 3.1   An outline of the communications system considered.

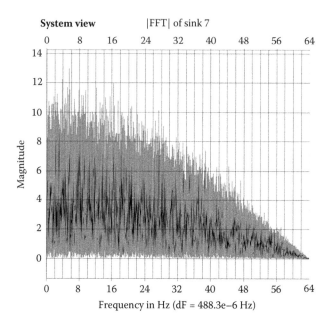

Figure 3.2   A view of the spectrum of the sparse component of the smart noise.

It follows from Equation 3.2.1 and Equation 3.2.2 that operations performed by token 0 and token 1 present the original time series as the sum of two other time series, which, presuming that consecutive samples of the original time series are uncorrelated, provides that at least the first two statistical momenta are the same for these two time series.

Other properties of these two time series, however, are different. The most noticeable difference is in their Fourier spectra. Figure 3.2 shows the spectrum of the output of token 1. Figure 3.3 shows the spectrum of the output of token 0. It is clear from these spectra that token 0 and Equation 3.2.1 describe a low-pass filter, whereas token 1 and Equation 3.2.2 describe a high-pass filter.

The random data streams generated by token 1 and token 0 are components for further generation of the smart noise. They enter a switch (token 2) with two states controlled by the output of token 15. Token 15 represents a source of the proprietary message to be transmitted. In this case, it is a PN sequence with the amplitude of 1 V and two levels, +1 and −1. Symbols at the output of token 15 are generated at the rate of 1 Hz. Accordingly, the two internal states of switch 2 are +1 and −1. The output of switch 2 is a sequence of 1-sec-long segments of the random data streams generated by token 0 and

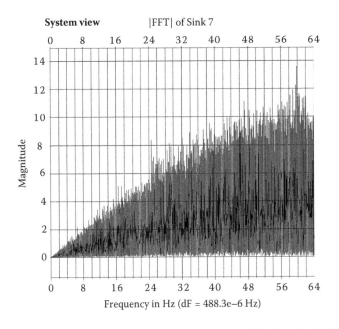

Figure 3.3   A view of the spectrum of the dense component of the smart noise.

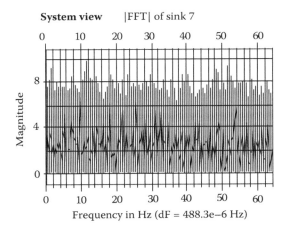

Figure 3.4   A view of the spectrum of the smart noise.

token 1. A typical spectrum of this output is shown in Figure 3.4. This spectrum is similar (i.e., exactly proportional with the proportionality coefficient of square root of 2) to that of the original time series generated by token 9, i.e., it is a typical white noise spectrum. However,

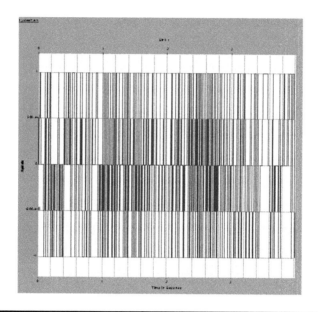

Figure 3.5   A snapshot of the smart noise.

this output has an internal structure mapped by the message generated by token 15. This is why one can regard it as a smart noise. A typical fragment of this output is shown in Figure 3.5. Four consecutive segments are shown; a careful look reveals that there are two sparser and two denser data segments.

The final element of the transmitter relevant to our study is token 21. This token generates a decoy signal that conceivably could be added to the smart noise if an additional level of protection is needed for the message to be transmitted. We will discuss the details of the operation relevant to token 21 later in this chapter. It will be assumed for now that the decoy signal generator is turned off.

Depending on the specifics of the system, the transmitter may be complemented by a band-pass filter whose purpose is to shape the spectral window at the edges. Also, if the smart noise is generated by combining more than two random data streams, the latter may have to be passed through a bank of detrenders.

Next, the smart noise enters the channel and is distorted (or, disguised) by the channel noise. In this study, an AWGN channel is assumed.

Next, the mixture of smart noise and channel noise enters the receiver. It is processed there by two sequences of tokens (token 8, token 4, token 7, token 3, and token 6; and token 10, token 12, token

14, token 11, and token 13). Token 8 performs the same operation as token 0. Similarly, token 10 performs the same operation as token 1. Token 4 and token 12 are cross-correlators with a window of 2. The outputs of these tokens, which are autocorrelation functions of the outputs from token 8 and token 10, are then each processed by a rectifier (i.e., an absolute value is taken). The rectifier outputs are then each smoothed out by a sequence of two averagers. We found that the best performance of this system is attained as the sizes (in samples) of the windows of token 3, token 11, token 6, and token 13 are mutually prime to the number of samples in one message symbol transmitted, i.e., 128. Specifically, the size of the window of token 3 and token 11 was 67, and the size of the window of token 6 and token 13 was 43 (see more about this in the next chapter). The outputs of token 6 and token 13 enter the comparator (token 5). The output of the comparator is either +1 or −1, depending on the result of the comparison, and it represents the proprietary message retrieved at the receiver.

The performance of this stealth communication system was analyzed by comparing symbols of the transmitted and received messages in the bit error rate (BER) token 19 after sampling these two messages at the rate of 1 Hz.

3.3 Test on Randomness

It was observed that transmitting the smart noise with a channel noise (CN) in the background may or may not be done in the stealth mode. Specifically, if the level of the SN is substantially higher than the level of the CN, then standard tests on randomness reveal an order in the structure of the mixture of SN and CN. However, at the SN-to-CN ratios (SNCNR) of the order of unity, the structure is hidden. This is illustrated by the results of simulations described below.

Fourier spectra of different mixtures of the SN and CN are shown in Figure 3.6 and Figure 3.7. These spectra were computed using 4096 samples. Figure 3.6 corresponds to the SNCNR value of 0 dB and Figure 3.7 to 20 dB. All these spectra look similar to that of white noise.

There are even more rigorous tests on randomness described in the following text [2]. Figure 3.8 is a snapshot of the AWGN, with a mean square deviation of 0.71 V, integrated over time. Figure 3.9 is a snapshot of the mixture of SN, with a mean square deviation of 0.71 V, and CN, with a mean square deviation of 0.71 V, integrated over time. The noise structures in both cases look similar.

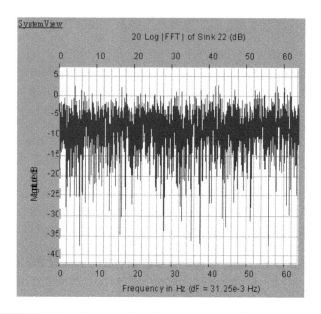

Figure 3.6 **A view of the spectrum of a mixture of the smart noise and the channel noise.**

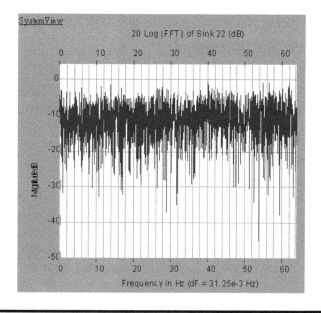

Figure 3.7 **A view of the spectrum of a mixture of the smart noise and the channel noise.**

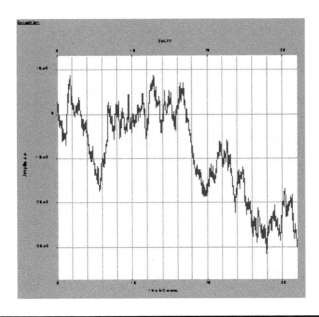

Figure 3.8 A snapshot of a pure channel noise integrated over time.

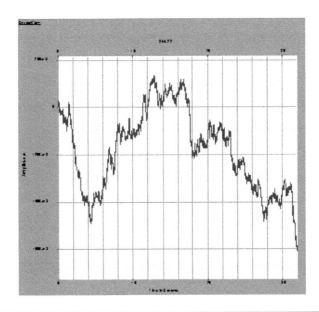

Figure 3.9 A snapshot of a mixture of the smart noise and the channel noise integrated over time.

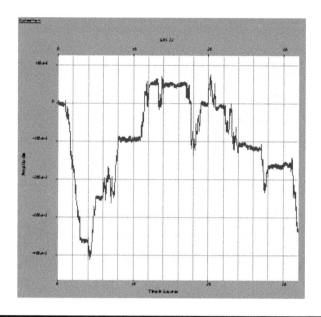

Figure 3.10 A snapshot of a mixture of the smart noise and the channel noise integrated over time.

Figure 3.10 is a snapshot of the mixture of SN, with a mean square deviation of 0.71 V, and CN, with a mean square deviation of 0.071 V, integrated over time. Comparing Figure 3.10 and Figure 3.8 reveals an ordered structure of the smart noise. Plateau intervals of the duration of approximately 1 s correspond to transmitting the sparse component of the SN, whereas steep ascends and descends between them correspond to transmitting the dense component of the SN. On the contrary, the AWGN structure does not contain such plateaus.

Figure 3.11 is a snapshot of the pure SN, with the mean square deviation of 0.71 V, integrated over time. One can see even more ordering than in the previous case considered.

A boundary value of the SNCNR separating the situations in which the structure of the SN with the CN in the background can and cannot be revealed is about 10 dB. This is shown in Figure 3.12, a snapshot of the mixture of SN, with a mean square deviation of 0.71 V, and CN, with a mean square deviation of 0.222 V, integrated over time.

3.4 BER Performance

We conducted a series of simulations to evaluate the performance of the stealth communication system described. Figure 3.13 presents

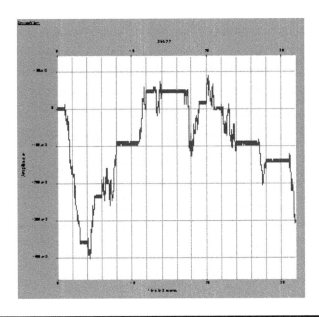

Figure 3.11   A snapshot of a pure smart noise integrated over time.

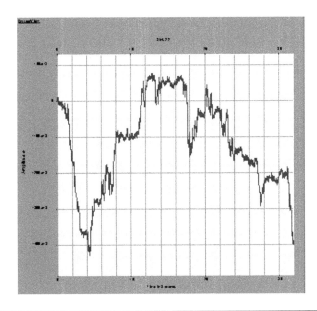

Figure 3.12   A snapshot of a mixture of the smart noise and the channel noise integrated over time.

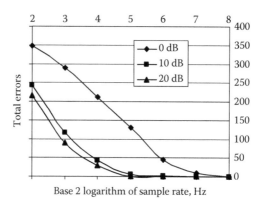

Figure 3.13   A plot presenting results of BER tests for the communication system considered.

results of several BER tests at different sample rates. It shows the total number of symbols in error versus the parameter n, in which the sample rate was determined as 2^n Hz. The source of the raw noise for generating the SN is a PN sequence with the amplitude of 1 V and the rate of 2^n Hz. The message to be transmitted is a PN sequence with an amplitude of 1 V and a symbol rate of 1 Hz. Each data point in Figure 3.13 was obtained by transmitting 1024 symbols. The sample rate considered ranged from 4 to 256 Hz. The BER performance improves as the sample rate increases. Specifically, at 128 Hz, 10 errors were detected at 0 dB and no errors were detected at 10 dB and 20 dB. At 256 Hz, no errors were detected in the entire range of SNCNR studied.

Figure 3.14 illustrates the effect of quantization errors on the BER performance. In this set of simulations, we used AWGN with a mean square deviation of 0.71 V as a channel noise. All other initial parameters are similar to the previous set of simulations. The system shown in Figure 3.1 was modified by including a quantizer following the adder 16. The SN was quantized with a maximum input of ±2 V; Figure 3.14 shows the total number of errors versus the number of bits quantized. The sufficient number of bits quantized equals 3, because retaining more than 3 bits does not change the BER performance.

Figure 3.15 describes the effect of a possible timing error in detecting the arrival of the SN at the receiver. To study this effect, the system shown in Figure 3.1 was modified by introducing a sample delay following the comparator 5. Figure 3.15 shows the total number of errors versus the delay in the arrival detection (in samples). The BER

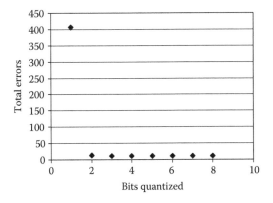

Figure 3.14 A plot presenting results of BER tests for the communication system considered.

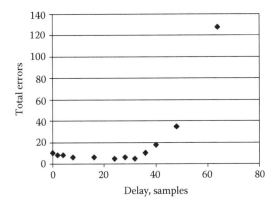

Figure 3.15 A plot presenting the results of BER tests for the communication system considered.

performance is about the same as the delay varies between 0 and 36 samples. This means that a timing error, as large as a quarter of the duration of one message symbol in the arrival detection, can be tolerated.

3.5 Using a Decoy Signal

A remarkable feature of this stealth communication system is that the SN can be complemented with a signal with a well-defined, even a

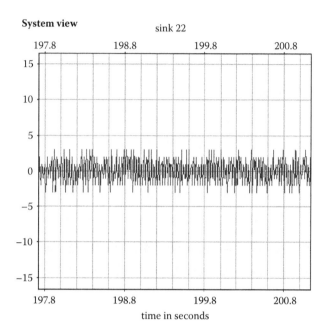

Figure 3.16   A snapshot of the mixture of the smart noise and a decoy chirp signal.

periodical structure. This would be a decoy signal aimed to disguise the presence of the SN. Note that this approach is completely opposite to the traditional one in which a lot of noise would be generated to disguise the presence of a nonrandom signal. Another remarkable feature of the method of adding the decoy signal to the SN is that it can be done not only without deteriorating but sometimes even enhancing the system performance.

Figure 3.16 and Figure 3.17 present the results of simulating the stealth communication system with the decoy signal feature turned on. The system shown in Figure 3.1 was modified by adding a source of a chirp of the magnitude of 3 V, the frequency range swept of 28 to 36 Hz, and the period of 0.031 sec. The channel noise was assumed to be very low, which in normal circumstances would not allow hiding the SN structure. However, as the magnitude of the decoy signal used here is substantially higher than the mean square deviation of the SN (0.71 V), variations in the decoy signal completely disguise the SN structure. It is also important to note that the preferred location of this decoy signal in the frequency spectrum is the central frequency of the spectral window used for transmission. It is well known that a possible inhomogeneity of the spectral density around the central frequency is

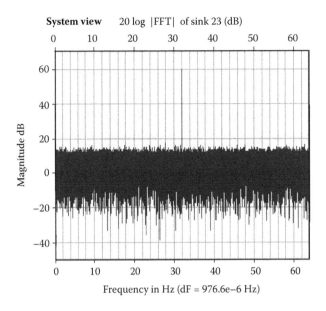

System view   20 log |FFT| of sink 23 (dB)

Frequency in Hz (dF = 976.6e–6 Hz)

Figure 3.17 A view of the spectrum of the smart noise and the decoy chirp signal.

considered a strong indication of the presence of an intelligent signal in the background noise [2]. However, in the case of using the SN (here, we specifically discuss a two-component SN), placing a narrow band decoy signal in the center of the spectral window does not corrupt the SN structure, because most of the energy carried by its components is localized in the lower half of the spectral window (for the sparse component) and in the higher half of the spectral window (for the dense component). As a result, there were no errors detected in transmitting the SN either with or without the decoy chirp signal. Figure 3.16 presents a snapshot of the mixture of SN and the chirp. Figure 3.17 presents the Fourier spectrum of this mixture. Looking at these figures, it seems obvious that someone had tried to transmit a narrowband information-bearing signal with a noise as a background. However, in fact, someone had tried to transmit an information-bearing noise with a nonrandom decoy signal as a background.

Even more impressive simulation results are presented in Figure 3.18 and Figure 3.19. In this case, transmitting the SN and a sine wave as a decoy signal was simulated. The magnitude of the sine wave was 11 V, the frequency was 32 Hz, and the phase was 50°. The snapshot of the mixture transmitted (Figure 3.18) shows an almost periodical signal. The spectrum measured at the receiver is shown in Figure 3.19.

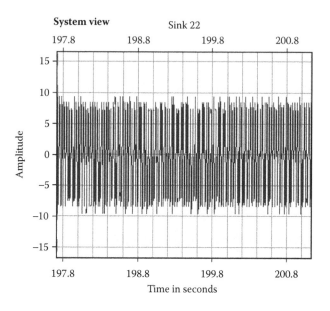

Figure 3.18 A snapshot of the mixture of the smart noise and a decoy harmonic signal.

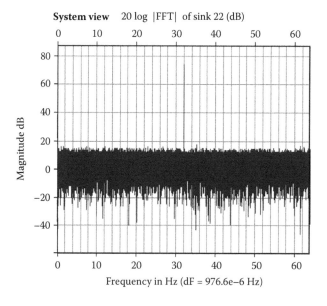

Figure 3.19 A view of the spectrum of the smart noise and the decoy harmonic signal.

No errors were detected. Moreover, we performed simulations in the presence of a channel AWGN with a mean square deviation of 0.71 V, and the BER performance was actually better in the presence of the harmonic decoy signal than in its absence.

An important conclusion is that one can use the SN for stealth transmission even when the channel noise is low if a sufficiently large and properly designed decoy signal is used in conjunction with the SN.

3.6 Conclusions

In this chapter, we introduced a method for proprietary data transmission. The essence of the method is transmitting a message over a communication channel using a smart noise having an internal structure associated with this message. This smart noise is a mixture of two components generated from the channel noise (or using a noise source with the properties of the channel noise; thus, implementing this method requires measurements of the spectrum of the channel noise) in accordance with Equation 3.2.1 and Equation 3.2.2. The smart noise generated in this manner has spectral properties matching those of the channel noise. Equation 3.2.1 and Equation 3.2.2 provide a "recipe" for an optimally disguised (spectrum-wise) information-bearing mixture of two noise-like components.

This smart noise can be combined with a nonrandom decoy signal. The frequency of the decoy signal should be carefully chosen. If the smart noise consists of two components, this frequency should be the central frequency of the spectral window used for transmission. If the smart noise consists of several components, and the spectra of these components are predominantly localized in adjacent sections of the spectral window used for transmission, this frequency should be chosen at the boundary of two adjacent sections of the spectral window.

References

1. Mitlin, V., Method of Determining the Quality of a Communication Channel, U.S. Patent Application No. 10/729,740, pending.
2. Masters, T., *Neural and Hybrid Algorithms for Time Series Prediction*, John Wiley & Sons, New York, 1995.
3. Proakis, J.G., *Digital Communications*, McGraw-Hill, New York, 1995.
4. Mitlin, V., Stealth Communication Method, U.S. Patent No. 10/817,869, 2004.

Chapter 4

Pulse Shape Optimization

4.1 Background

This chapter describes a method of pulse shaping or, more specifically, of generating low-complexity, spectrally efficient pulses for digital communications.

In digital communications, the data transmission is performed, in the most basic pulse amplitude modulation (PAM) scenario, by creating a train of identical pulses and multiplying each pulse by a number representing a symbol of an information-bearing sequence to be transmitted. The Shannon theory establishes a relationship between the data rate of a communication channel, the signal power, and the bandwidth. Specifically, both an increase in the power and the bandwidth yield an increase in the channel data rate. An ideal situation would be if one were allowed to increase the power of the pulse used for data transmission as well as its bandwidth as much as one desires to achieve the required data rate. Then one would transmit a sequence of very tall and narrow pulses. However, such pulses should not be used in reality, as there are severe restrictions on the power level of a pulse as well as on the bandwidth it occupies. Therefore, such a sequence has to be passed through a filter that modifies the pulse shape and, for a given energy of the pulse, reduces its effective bandwidth [1,3]. Designing bandwidth-efficient pulses is an important problem, particularly in wireless applications where the bandwidth occupancy

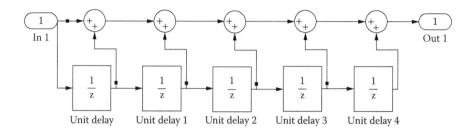

Figure 4.1 An example of a sliding adder with five binary adders and five unit delay elements.

affects the total number of users in the spectral window allocated for a given service provider. Methods associated with the pulse choice are referred to as pulse shaping methods.

There are several standard methods of pulse shaping currently used. The most popular pulses are rectangular, Bartlett, Hanning, Blackman, and Hamming. Of these five pulses, the first two should be separated from the last three, the separation criterion being the processing complexity. Specifically, a rectangular pulse is created by passing a unit area impulse through a sliding adder like the one shown in Figure 4.1. The Bartlett pulse is created by passing a unit area impulse through a sequence of two identical sliding adders. The complexity of circuitry associated with generating Hanning, Hamming, and Blackman pulses is substantially higher, because it also includes several multipliers.

In the following text, we describe a method of generating pulses with enhanced bandwidth occupancy [4]. A bandwidth occupancy criterion in the form of a variational problem is introduced. This problem has an analytical solution yielding an optimum termed the *SO-pulse*. A low-complexity approximation of this pulse is given by the logistic equation and is termed the *L-pulse*. Finally, a new trapezoidal pulse termed the *phi-pulse* is introduced. The phi-pulse provides an optimum for the bandwidth occupancy criterion on a subclass of pulses generated by passing a unit area impulse through a sequence of sliding adders. Simulations of bit error rate (BER) tests show that these new pulses are superior to the standard ones used in digital communications.

4.2 Pulse Shape Optimization Criterion

A natural requirement of a good pulse is its spectrum confinement. An intuitive notion of a spectrally confined signal comes from observing

0

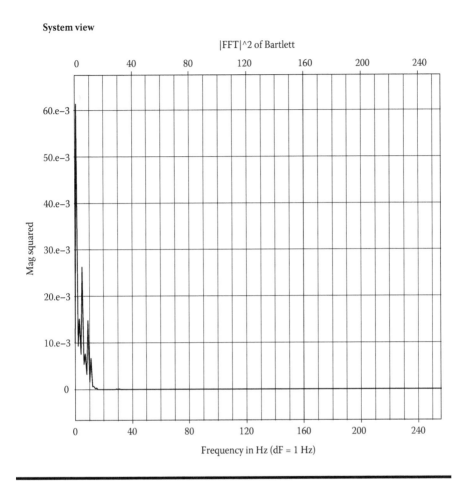

Figure 4.2   The spectral density of the Bartlett pulse.

the signal spectral density. The spectral density of a good pulse should be concentrated in a relatively small vicinity of zero frequency. Figure 4.2 and Figure 4.3 present the spectral densities of the Bartlett and Blackman pulses. From looking at these spectra, the Bartlett pulse seems to contain a larger portion of its total energy in the same vicinity of zero frequency than the Blackman pulse. This observation can be quantified, for instance, as follows: one can integrate the spectral density from zero to a given frequency, plot the result as a function of frequency, and overlay it with its mean value. The result is shown in Figure 4.4 and Figure 4.5; the frequency at the point of intersection can be used as a measure of spectrum confinement. Thus, with respect to its spectrum confinement, the Bartlett pulse is better than the Blackman pulse.

System view

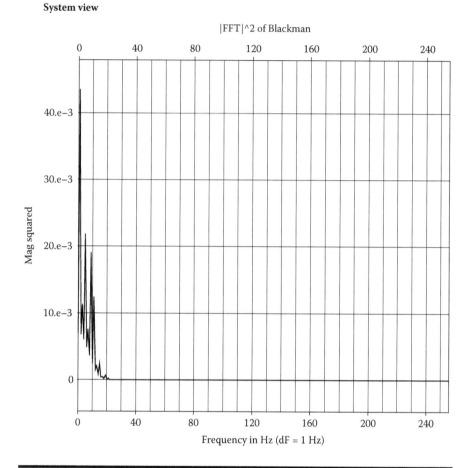

Figure 4.3   **The spectral density of the Blackman pulse.**

The measure of spectrum confinement discussed earlier is termed the *spectral width*. The spectral width is the optimization criterion to be used in the following text. As this quantity is a functional of the spectral density of a signal, it is more convenient to use an equivalent formulation in terms of the signal itself as follows:

$$W^* = \min W, \quad W = \sqrt{J}, \quad J = \frac{\int_0^T \left(\frac{ds}{dt}\right)^2 dt}{\int_0^T s^2 dt} \tag{4.2.1}$$

System view

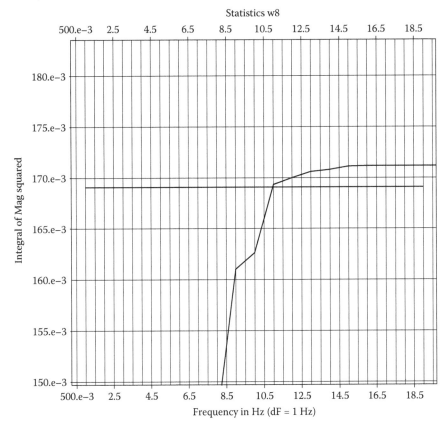

Figure 4.4 A geometrical construction used for determining the spectral width of the Bartlett pulse.

Equation 4.2.1 states that J, the square of the effective bandwidth W occupied by a signal s(t) with a period of T, has to be minimized. The rest of the chapter describes pulse shapes that are optimal with respect to the criterion (Equation 4.2.1).

It should be noted that a general expression for J is more complex. Specifically,

$$J = \frac{T \sum_{i=1}^{N} a_i^2 \int_0^T \left(\frac{ds}{dt}\right)^2 dt - \left(\sum_{i=1}^{N} a_i \int_0^T \frac{ds}{dt} dt\right)^2}{T \sum_{i=1}^{N} a_i^2 \int_0^T s^2 dt} \qquad (4.2.2)$$

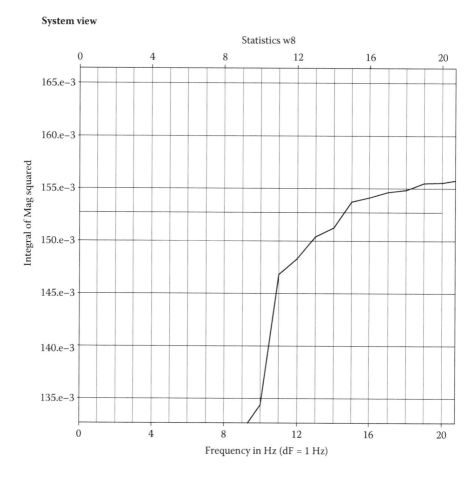

Figure 4.5 A geometrical construction used for determining the spectral width of the Blackman pulse.

where the summation is taken over the index i enumerating the information-bearing sequence {a_i}. It will be assumed in the subsequent analysis that each pulse vanishes at the ends of the interval (0,T). Then, Equation 4.2.2 reduces to the much simpler Equation 4.2.1.

4.3 SO-Pulse and L-Pulse

Generally, the functional J has to be minimized for all pulses of a given area defined in the interval (0, T) and vanishing at the endpoints of this interval. The exact solution of the optimization problem (Equation 4.2.1) is obtained using standard methods of the calculus of variations [2]. The optimal pulse has the following continuous representation:

$$0 \leq t \leq T: \quad s = A \sin \frac{\pi t}{T} \qquad (4.3.1)$$

where A is the pulse magnitude. This pulse is termed the *SO-pulse*, where SO stands for "spectrally optimal." One can see that the SO-pulse is a version of the root-raised cosine pulse.

A simulator was developed to study this optimization problem. Each run started with a slightly perturbed rectangular pulse shape of height p and width n. At each iteration, two points from the interval (1, n) were chosen at random. The pulse value in the first point was decreased by 1, and the pulse value in the second point was increased by 1. Then, the J value was computed for the modified pulse; if the new value was smaller than the old one, the new pulse shape was processed in the same manner; otherwise, the proposed pulse shape was rejected. To avoid falling into a local minimum, a version of the simulated annealing method was implemented. Specifically, if the J value remained the same for a certain number of trials, the value of a local increment in the pulse shape was doubled, then tripled, and so on. The MatLab script used is presented in Appendix B.

The results at n = 50 are shown in Figure 4.6 through Figure 4.10. The optimal shape depended on the value of the pulse area that was invariant in each run. At large p/n, the optimum pulse shape looks similar to those shown in Figure 4.9 and Figure 4.10. After the optimal pulse shapes were normalized by their maximum values, the same smooth prolate SO-pulse given by Equation 4.3.1 was obtained.

It was found that the optimal pulse shape is almost perfectly described (i.e., with the deviation of J from its optimal value not exceeding 1 percent) by the logistic equation:

$$0 \leq t \leq T: \quad s = A \frac{4Tt - 4t^2}{T^2} \qquad (4.3.2)$$

This pulse is termed the *L-pulse*, where L stands for "logistic."

At small p/n (0.3 to 0.5; Figure 4.6 to Figure 4.7), the optimum would look like a symmetrical trapezoidal pulse. Further increase in p/n smoothed the corners of the optimum pulse.

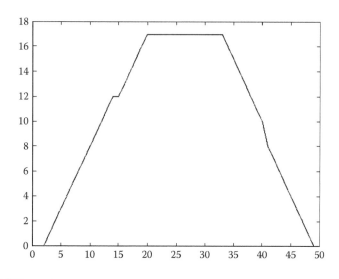

Figure 4.6 An optimum pulse shape obtained in computer simulations at p/n = 0.3.

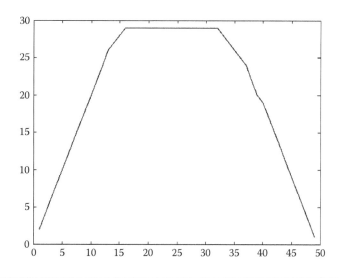

Figure 4.7 An optimum pulse shape obtained in computer simulations at p/n = 0.5.

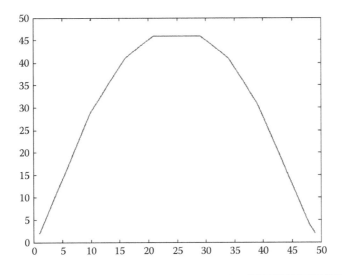

Figure 4.8 An optimum pulse shape obtained in computer simulations at p/n = 0.7.

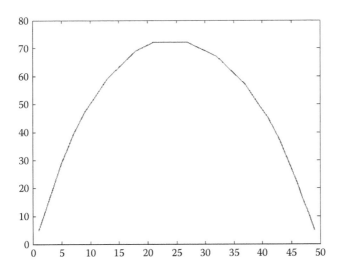

Figure 4.9 An optimum pulse shape obtained in computer simulations at p/n = 3.

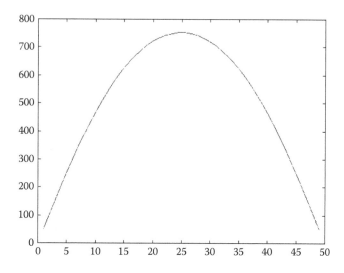

Figure 4.10 An optimum pulse shape obtained in computer simulations at p/n = 100.

4.4 Phi-Pulse

Results of simulations shown earlier demonstrate that the narrower the class of pulses on which J is minimized (or, equivalently, the smaller the value of p/n), the more the optimal pulse shape looks trapezoidal. This section presents a theory of the pulse that minimizes Equation 4.2.1 on a certain class of pulses. Each of these pulses is generated via passing a unit area pulse through a sequence of sliding adders (SAS). In addition, a requirement of the same processing complexity is imposed on the set of pulses on which the optimum is sought; specifically, the sum of the lengths (in samples) of all the adders in each sequence is equal to the same value n. This is a broad class of pulses; the rectangular pulse and the Bartlett pulse belong to it.

Consider the subclass of pairs of adders with the total length of n. If the length of the first sliding adder is $m < n/2$, the length of the second sliding adder is $n - m$. A typical pulse generated in this way is shown in Figure 4.11. It is symmetrical and trapezoidal with height m, lower base length n, and upper base length $n - 2m + 2$ (here, for convenience, consider the case of the sampling rate of unity). This can be formalized as follows:

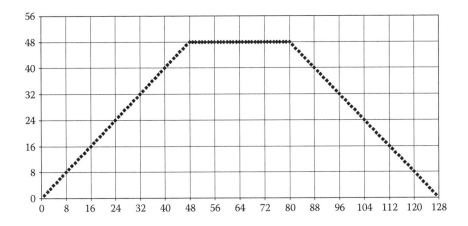

Figure 4.11   The phi-pulse at n = 128.

$$0 \le i \le m: \quad s = \frac{i}{m}$$

$$m < i < n - m: \quad s = 1 \tag{4.4.1}$$

$$n - m \le i \le n: \quad s = \frac{n - i}{m}$$

For the case considered, the expression for J in Equation 4.2.1 can be written out explicitly in a discrete form:

$$J = \frac{2m}{\left(\dfrac{m(m + 1)(2m + 1)}{3} + m^2(n - 2m - 1) \right)}$$

$$= \frac{6}{\left(-4m^2 + 3nm + 1 \right)} \tag{4.4.2}$$

Figure 4.12 shows the dependency of the base 10 logarithm of J versus m at n = 128.

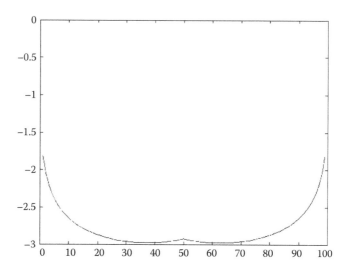

Figure 4.12   The dependency of the base 10 logarithm of J on m at n = 128.

The denominator in Equation 4.4.2 is maximized at:

$$m^* = \frac{3n}{8} \qquad (4.4.3)$$

As m is an integer, Equation 4.4.3 has to be rewritten as:

$$m^* = \left[\frac{3n}{8} \right] \qquad (4.4.4)$$

In Equation 4.4.4, [x] denotes the closest integer to a given real number x. Table 4.1 shows how Equation 4.4.4 works. When the remainder of dividing n by 8 is 0, 1, 3, and 6, the right-hand side of Equation 4.4.3 is rounded down; when this remainder is 2, 5, and 7, the right-hand side of Equation 4.4.3 is rounded up; finally, when this remainder is 4, the right-hand side of Equation 4.4.3 may be rounded up or down with the same effect and, to be specific, it is rounded down in this case.

Introducing Equation 4.4.3 into Equation 4.4.2 yields the minimum value of J on the subclass considered:

$$J^* = \frac{96}{9n^2 + 16} \qquad (4.4.5)$$

Table 4.1   The Round-Off Table for Calculating the m Value of a Phi-Pulse

n%8	[3n/8]-3n%8
0	0
1	0
2	1
3	0
4	0(1)
5	1
6	0
7	1

Now it is easy to generalize the results obtained to the case of an arbitrary sampling frequency f and the pulse period T. The effective bandwidth occupied by the optimal pulse is given by the following formula:

$$W^* = \sqrt{\frac{96f^2}{9T^2f^2 + 16}} \xrightarrow{f \to \infty} \frac{\sqrt{\left(\frac{32}{3}\right)}}{T} \approx \frac{3.27}{T} \qquad (4.4.6)$$

Compare the results obtained for the optimal trapezoidal pulse to those for the Bartlett and rectangular pulses. For the Bartlett pulse, the J value is obtained by introducing m = n/2 into Equation 4.4.2. This yields:

$$J' = \frac{12}{n^2 + 2} \qquad (4.4.7)$$

Combining Equation 4.4.5 and Equation 4.4.7 yields an expression for the effective bandwidth ratio of the optimal trapezoidal pulse to the Bartlett pulse, X:

$$X = \sqrt{\frac{8T^2f^2 + 16}{9T^2f^2 + 16}} \xrightarrow{f \to \infty} \sqrt{\frac{8}{9}} \approx 0.94 \qquad (4.4.8)$$

In the limit of large sampling frequencies, the bandwidth reduction is about 6 percent. For the rectangular pulse, the J value is obtained by introducing m = 1 into Equation 4.4.2. This yields:

$$J'' = \frac{2}{n - 1} \tag{4.4.9}$$

Combining Equation 4.4.9 and Equation 4.4.5 yields an expression for the effective bandwidth ratio of the optimal trapezoidal pulse to the rectangular pulse, Y:

$$Y = 6\sqrt{\frac{Tf - 1}{9T^2f^2 + 16}} \xrightarrow{f \to \infty} 0 \tag{4.4.10}$$

In the limit of large sampling frequencies, the ratio of bandwidth values of the optimal trapezoidal pulse to the rectangular pulse tends to zero.

Figure 4.11 shows the optimal trapezoidal pulse at n = 128. We termed it the *phi-pulse* because n/(n − m*) = 1.60 is very close to the golden ratio φ = 1.62. Its continuous representation is:

$$0 \le t \le \frac{3T}{8} : \quad s = \frac{8At}{3T}$$

$$\frac{3T}{8} < t < \frac{5T}{8} : \quad s = A \tag{4.4.11}$$

$$\frac{5T}{8} \le t \le T : \quad s = \frac{8A}{3} - \frac{8At}{3T}$$

Table 4.2 shows typical parameters of the phi-pulse at n equal to the first few powers of two, including the number of binary adders and unit delay elements in each of the two sliding adders needed to generate the pulse.

The phi-pulse is optimal on the subclass of pulses generated by passing a unit area pulse through a sequence of two sliding adders. A Matlab code was written to verify the derivations; it yielded the same conclusion for n as large as 256. Naturally, the following question arises: what is the optimal pulse shape on the subclass of pulses generated by passing a unit area pulse through a sequence of more

Table 4.2   Parameters of Phi-Pulses at Different Values of n

n, Samples	m*	Number of Adders/Delays in the First Sliding Summer	Number of Adders/Delays in the Second Sliding Summer
4	2	1	1
8	3	2	4
16	6	5	9
32	12	11	19
64	24	23	39
128	48	47	79
256	96	95	159

Table 4.3   J Values of Various Pulses Studied at Different Values of n

n	J, phi	J, Bartlett	J, Hanning	J, Blackman	J, Rectang.	J, L
8	0.163	0.1818	0.1953	0.2614	0.2857	0.1538
16	0.0414	0.0465	0.0507	0.0686	0.1333	0.0389
32	0.0104	0.0117	0.0128	0.0174	0.0645	0.01
64	0.0026	0.0029	0.0032	0.0044	0.0317	0.0024
128	6.50E-04	7.32E-04	8.03E-04	0.0011	1.57E-02	6.09E-04

than two sliding adders with the total length of n? We could not solve this problem analytically; thus, two more programs were written to determine the optimal shape when a generating sequence consisted of three and four adders (see MatLab scripts in Appendix B). The optimal shape in these two cases was again the phi-pulse. This is verified for n as large as 256. Of course, a checkup of this statement cannot be performed for any n but analytical and numerical verifications performed indicate that the phi-pulse is optimal on the whole class of pulses considered.

Table 4.3 presents the J values for various pulses considered in this study. Results for the SO-pulse are not presented, as they are almost identical to those of the L-pulse. In terms of spectrum confinement, the pulses, arranged in descending order of quality, are the L-pulse, phi-pulse, Bartlett pulse, Hanning pulse, Blackman pulse, and rectangular pulse.

Table 4.4   Peak-to-Average Power Ratios for Various Pulses Studied

PAPR, phi	PAPR, Bartlett	PAPR, Hanning	PAPR, Blackman	PAPR, SO	PAPR , L
2	3	2.667	3.283	2	1.875

Table 4.4 is a table presenting peak-to-average power ratios (PAPRs) for various pulses studied. The L-pulse has the lowest PAPR, the phi-pulse and the SO-pulse are next, followed by Hanning, Bartlett, and Blackman pulses, respectively.

4.5   BER Test

The next question to answer is how the difference in J values for two given pulses reflects in their comparative transmission properties. To answer this question, Matlab simulators of the BER test were developed for each pulse considered. Such a simulator is shown in Figure 4.13.

A given pulse with a period of 1 s is generated in the subsystem Out2. This subsystem is shown in more detail in Figure 4.14 for the case of generating a train of phi-pulses. It consists of a unit area pulse train generator, followed by two sliding adders and an amplifier (gain). The pulse generated is sampled at the rate of 128 Hz and multiplied by a symbol from an information-bearing binary sequence with a rate of 1 Hz. Then it is passed through the *additive white Gaussian noise* (AWGN) channel. The optimal correlator type of receiver was implemented, i.e., the signal corrupted with noise is multiplied by the exact replica of the pulse and integrated over the pulse period. The result is put through a slicer, downsampled by 128, and compared to the transmitted symbol of the information-bearing sequence. To have a fair basis for comparison of the performance of different pulses, the pulse power was the same in all simulations, e.g., 0.375. Three cases were considered, e.g., the AWGN variance was equal to 8, 12, and 16. In the first case, the transmission of 50,000 bits was simulated; in the other two cases, 10,000 bits. Not only was the effect of noise on the BER analyzed, but also the effect of the timing error. This was done by introducing the delay element in the channel part of the simulator. The BER test was run at timing error values equal to 0, 8, 16, 24, and 32 samples, which is equivalent to 0, 1/16, 1/8, 3/16, and 1/4 of the pulse period. The results are shown in Figure 4.15 to Figure 4.17, respectively. These figures show that the L-pulse and the phi-pulse are superior to the Bartlett, Hanning, and Blackman pulses. This becomes apparent, as the timing error increases.

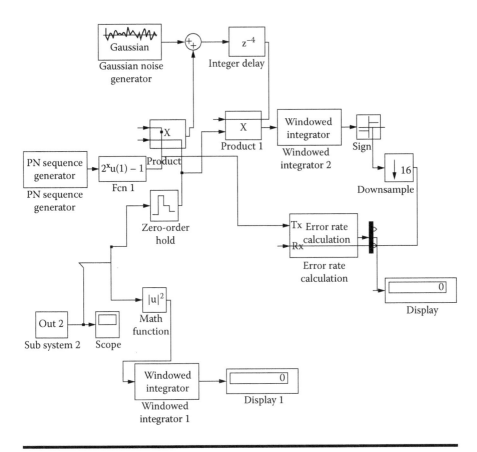

Figure 4.13 A schematic representation of the BER test simulator used.

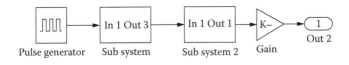

Figure 4.14 A schematic representation of a subsystem of the simulator shown in Figure 4.13.

There is a strong quantitative correlation between the J value of a pulse and the BER it yields. More specifically, it was observed that for the same level of noise and the same timing error, the ratio of BERs of two pulses compared is approximately equal to the ratio of their J values, as illustrated in Figure 4.18. This figure shows the number of bit errors in 10,000 bits transmitted at the timing error of 1/4 of the pulse period versus the J values in the case of AWGN variance of 12

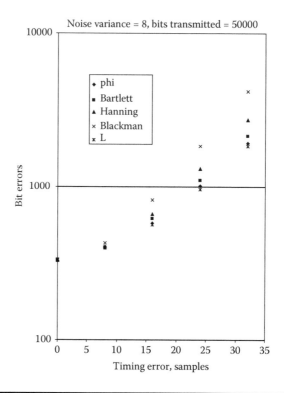

Figure 4.15   A plot showing results of BER test simulations for various pulses studied in AWGN channel with noise variance of 8; 50,000 bits transmitted.

(diamonds) and 16 (triangles), respectively. The dependency in both cases is approximately linear. This allows one to propose a simple method of comparing the average BER performances, over the existing range of timing errors, of two pulses without running an actual BER test. Thus, estimating the BER of a new pulse can be done by multiplying the BER of a "cataloged" pulse by the ratio of the J value of the first pulse to that of the second pulse.

4.6 Approximation of Pulses by SAS

This section describes how to approximate some pulse-generating circuits by SAS. SAS were introduced earlier when the phi-pulse shape was obtained. Binary SAS are equivalent to piecewise-linear approximations, triple SAS to piecewise-quadratic, quaternary SAS to piecewise-cubic approximations, and so on. This problem is important

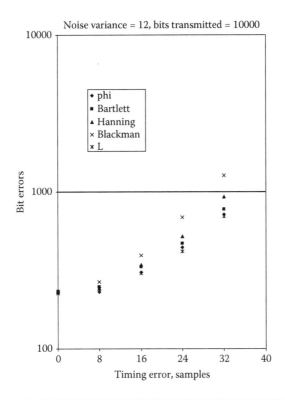

Figure 4.16 A plot showing results of BER test simulations for various pulses studied in AWGN channel with noise variance of 12; 10,000 bits transmitted.

because, as mentioned earlier, SAS are represented in hardware by low-complexity devices that do not include multipliers.

Several Matlab codes were developed for solving this problem. These codes use the following algorithm: they go through all of the SAS of a total length n trying to minimize the square deviation between a shape generated by a given SAS and the pulse shape approximated.

The results are impressive. Figure 4.19 shows the comparison between an exact shape of the Hanning pulse and its SAS approximation at n = 64. It is hard to tell where the real Hanning pulse is and where is its approximation. Apparently, the optimal approximation in this case corresponds to the following sequence of adder lengths: 12, 21, and 32. It is interesting that the increase in the number of sliding adders in the SAS from three to four or five does not modify this result. It is generally found that the best SAS approximation of the Hanning pulse is attained on the sequence of three sliding adders of the lengths

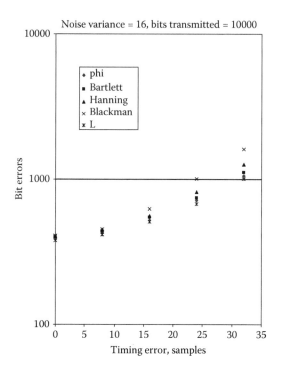

Figure 4.17   A plot showing results of BER test simulations for various pulses studied in AWGN channel with noise variance of 16; 10,000 bits transmitted.

approximately equal to n/2, n/3, and n/6. In other words, the optimal lengths form approximately the following proportion: 1:2:3.

Figure 4.20 shows the comparison between an exact shape of the Blackman pulse and its SAS approximation at n = 64. Again, it is hard to tell where the real Blackman pulse is and where is its approximation. The optimal approximation in this case corresponds to the following sequence of adder lengths: 22, 22, 15, and 7. Here also, the increase in the number of adders in the SAS from four to five does not modify this result. Generally, it is found that the best SAS approximation of the Blackman pulse is attained on the sequence of four sliding adders of the lengths approximately equal to n/3, n/3, n/8, and 5n/24. The optimal lengths form approximately the following proportion: 8:8:3:5.

Of course, the best SAS approximation of L-pulse and SO-pulse is the phi-pulse.

It is also possible to implement the L-pulse without using multipliers, although the appropriate circuit should include a rectifier (taking an absolute value) in addition to several unit delay elements and binary

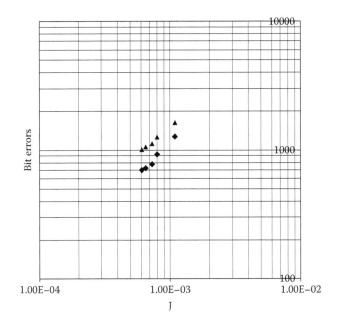

Figure 4.18 The J dependence of the total number of bit errors in 10,000 bits transmitted in a BER test on AWGN channel with noise variance of 12 (diamonds) and 16 (triangles), for various pulses studied.

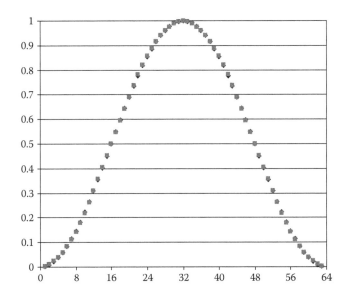

Figure 4.19 A plot showing the Hanning pulse (diamonds) and its SAS approximation (squares) at n = 64.

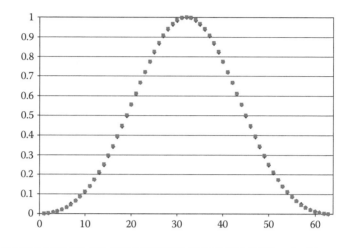

Figure 4.20 **A plot showing the Blackman pulse (diamonds) and its SAS approximation (squares) at n = 64.**

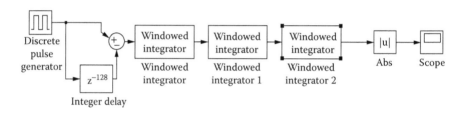

Figure 4.21 **A schematic representation of a subsystem of the simulator shown in Figure 4.13 responsible for pulse generation (case of an L-pulse is shown).**

adders. For n = 128, such a circuit is shown in Figure 4.21. This circuit was actually used in the BER test simulator, generating a train of L-pulses with a magnitude of one and a period of one. The circuit includes three window integrators of the lengths 64, 64, and 127 samples; a rectifier; a delay element of the length of 128 samples; and a discrete pulse generator with the magnitude of 512, period of 256 samples, phase delay of 63 samples, and pulse width of 1 sample. It generates the pulse train shown in Figure 4.22. This circuit starts generating the right kind of pulses after 256 initial samples. Generating a train of L-pulses of the magnitude of one and the period of one on the sampling rate of an even f requires a circuit with three window integrators of the lengths of f/2, f/2, and f − 1 samples; a rectifier, a

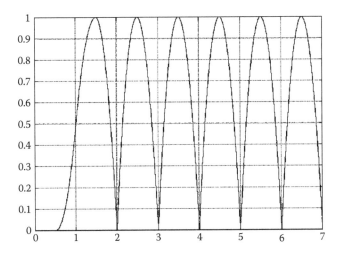

Figure 4.22   **An initial part of an L-pulse train generated using the subsystem shown in Figure 4.21.**

delay element of the length of f samples; and a discrete pulse generator with the magnitude of 4*f, period of 2*f samples, phase delay of (f/2) – 1 sample, and a pulse width of 1 sample. Also, if using a sliding adder instead of each of the window integrators, the circuit should include an amplifier (a gain element) with the value of $1/f^3$.

At n = 127 (or, equivalently, at T = 1 s and the sampling rate of 1/128 Hz), the parameters of the circuit shown in Figure 4.21 should be modified. The circuit should include three window integrators of the lengths 63, 64, and 127 samples; a rectifier; a delay element of the length of 127 samples; and a discrete pulse generator with the magnitude of 508, period of 254 samples, phase delay of 63 samples, and pulse width of 1 sample. To generate a train of L-pulses of the magnitude of one and the period of one on the sampling rate of an odd f, requires a circuit with three window integrators of the lengths of (f + 1)/2, (f – 1)/2, f samples; a rectifier, a delay element of the length of f samples; and a discrete pulse generator with the magnitude of 4*f, period of 2*f samples, phase delay of (f – 1)/2 samples, and a pulse width of 1 sample. Also, if using a sliding adder instead of each of the window integrators, the circuit should include an amplifier (gain) with the value of $1/f^3$.

BER test simulators were developed for SAS approximations of the Hanning and Blackman pulses. The results obtained were almost identical (i.e., differed by no more than three or four errors in each run) to those obtained for the original Hanning and Blackman pulses.

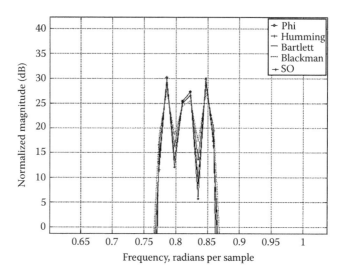

Figure 4.23 The spectral density of a sum of three sine waves with close frequencies obtained by using various pulses studied as windowing functions.

4.7 Data Windows Corresponding to the Pulses Introduced

Compare the new pulses to the existing ones with respect to their windowing properties. If a fragment of a time series is used to analyze its spectrum, it is multiplied by a windowing function, and the spectrum of the product is then evaluated. A standard test of quality of a windowing function consists of evaluating a spectrum of a sum of several sine waves with close frequencies using a short fragment of the corresponding time series. Figure 4.23 shows the spectral density of a sum of three sine waves of a unit magnitude with frequencies 1.135, 1.13, and 1.125 rad per sample using 512 samples. The L-pulse is the best and the phi-pulse is the second best with respect to distinguishing between the peaks of the spectral density corresponding to these sine waves.

Another test of quality of a windowing function consists in evaluating its performance deterioration after applying a quantizer of a certain resolution q to its values. Figure 4.24 to Figure 4.29 show spectral densities of the aforementioned sum of sine waves without quantization (circles) and upon applying a quantizer with the resolution

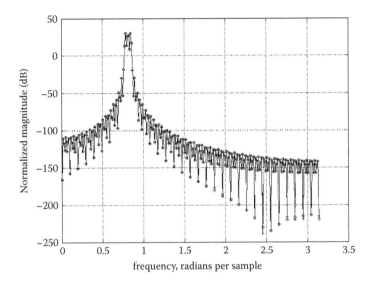

Figure 4.24 The spectral density of a sum of three sine waves with close frequencies obtained by using the phi-pulse as a windowing function, without quantization ("o") and with quantization level of 1E-5 ("+").

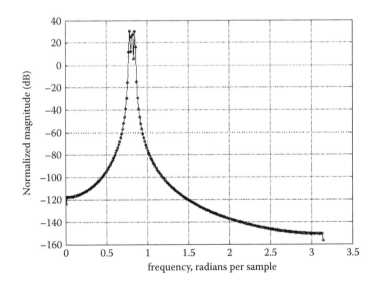

Figure 4.25 The spectral density of a sum of three sine waves with close frequencies obtained by using the SO-pulse as a windowing function, without quantization ("o") and with quantization level of 1E-5 ("+").

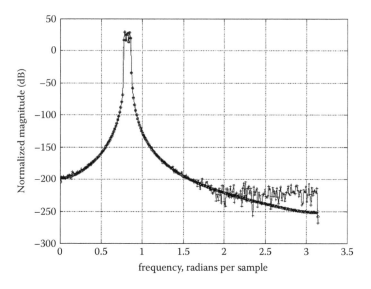

Figure 4.26 The spectral density of a sum of three sine waves with close frequencies obtained by using the Hanning pulse as a windowing function, without quantization ("o") and with quantization level of 1E-5 ("+").

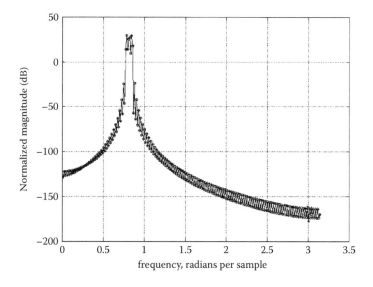

Figure 4.27 The spectral density of a sum of three sine waves with close frequencies obtained by using the Bartlett pulse as a windowing function, without quantization ("o") and with quantization level of 1E-5 ("+").

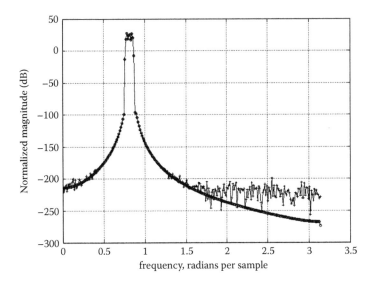

Figure 4.28 The spectral density of a sum of three sine waves with close frequencies obtained by using the Blackman pulse as a windowing function, without quantization ("o") and with quantization level of 1E-5 ("+").

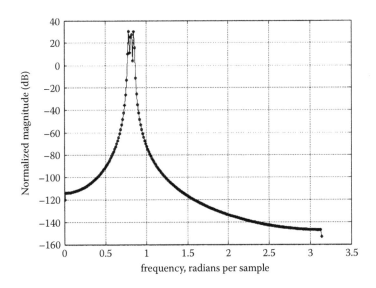

Figure 4.29 The spectral density of a sum of three sine waves with close frequencies obtained by using the L-pulse as a windowing function, without quantization ("o") and with quantization level of 1E-5 ("+").

of 1E-5, for phi-pulse, SO-pulse, Hanning pulse, Bartlett pulse, Blackman pulse, and L-pulse, respectively. This test shows that quantization does not affect the phi-pulse, SO-pulse, or the L-pulse, unlike the Hanning and Blackman pulses.

4.8 Raised Pulses

Finally, it is possible to introduce "raised" pulses using their "nonraised" versions presented earlier. Specifically, the well-known Hamming pulse can be obtained from another well-known Hanning pulse by multiplying the latter by 0.92 and adding 0.08. A similar transformation applied to the phi-pulse, L-pulse, and SO-pulse yields the following continuous representations of their raised counterparts:

$$0 \leq t \leq \frac{3T}{8} \; : \quad s = 0.08A + \frac{736At}{300T}$$

$$\frac{3T}{8} < t < \frac{5T}{8} \; : \quad s = A \qquad\qquad (4.8.1)$$

$$\frac{5T}{8} \leq t \leq T : \quad s = \frac{760A}{300} - \frac{736At}{300T}$$

$$0 \leq t \leq T : \quad s = 0.08A + 3.68A\frac{Tt - t^2}{T^2} \qquad\qquad (4.8.2)$$

$$0 \leq t \leq T : \quad s = 0.08A + 0.92\,A\sin\frac{\pi t}{T} \qquad\qquad (4.8.3)$$

Figure 4.30 and Figure 4.31 present spectral densities of a sum of three sine waves with frequencies specified earlier without quantization ("o") and with quantization level of 1E-5 ("+"), for the Hamming pulse and raised L-pulse, respectively.

Depending on specific requirements of a communication system, a designer should choose one of the new pulses described in this chapter based on their PAPR values, J values, BER performance, and processing complexity.

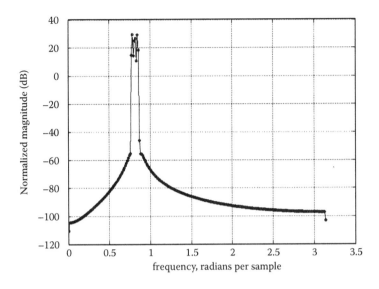

Figure 4.30 The spectral density of a sum of three sine waves with close frequencies obtained by using the Hamming pulse as a windowing function, without quantization ("o") and with quantization level of 1E-5 ("+").

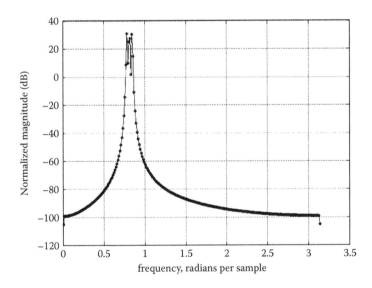

Figure 4.31 The spectral density of a sum of three sine waves with close frequencies obtained by using the raised L-pulse as a windowing function, without quantization ("o") and with quantization level of 1E-5 ("+").

4.9 Conclusions

In this chapter we presented a methodology for generating low-complexity, spectrally efficient pulses for digital communications, which includes obtaining these pulses in accordance with an optimization criterion and using them for data transmission and signal processing.

The generation of spectrally efficient pulses in accordance with an optimization criterion is accomplished by minimizing the pulse spectral width for pulses of predefined period and area. The optimal pulse termed the SO-pulse has the continuous representation (Equation 4.3.1). A low-complexity approximation of this pulse has the continuous representation (Equation 4.3.2) and is termed the L-pulse.

We also consider the question about the shape of the pulse that is optimal for a certain class of pulses. The pulses of this class are generated by passing a unit area impulse through a sequence of sliding adders (SAS) with a predefined length; each of these sliding adders is a sequence of connected pairs; each of these includes a binary adder and a unit delay element; and the aforementioned length is the number of connected pairs in all of the sliding adders. It was found that the optimal pulse for this class is a simple trapezoidal pulse with the continuous representation (Equation 4.4.11).

This is an important result for the following reason: it shows that if one uses a sequence of sliding adders in a digital signal processing line, then, for a given complexity of this sequence, the optimal sequence consists just of two sliding adders, as described by Equation 4.4.11. For this reason, it is not necessary to use any more complex combinations of sliding adders because it will not do any good.

It was shown that SAS can be successfully used as low-complexity circuits to approximate existing, commonly used pulses. Particularly, it was shown how to approximate the Hanning and the Blackman pulses. An SAS approximation of the L-pulse was also described.

The new pulses introduced in this chapter can be used not only in digital communications but also in data processing as windowing functions/filters.

Simulations of data transmission and tests for windowing functions used in digital signal processing were performed. They showed that the new pulses were superior to the standard ones used in digital communications.

We also introduced a method of comparing the BER performance of two given pulses without performing BER tests by estimating the ratio of the BER values of these two pulses as the ratio of their spectral widths.

References

1. Proakis, J.G., *Digital Communications*, 3rd ed., McGraw-Hill, New York, 1995, pp. 233–248.
2. Korn, G.A., Korn, T.M., *Mathematical Handbook for Scientists and Engineers*, Dover, New York, 2000, pp. 344–356.
3. Rorabaugh, C.B., *DSP Primer*, McGraw-Hill, New York, 1998, pp. 181–205.
4. Mitlin, V., Spectrally Efficient Pulse Shaping Method, Patent Application No. 10/871,064, 2004.

Chapter 5

Optimal Phase Shifters for Peak-to-Average Power Ratio Reduction in Multicarrier Communication Systems

5.1 Background

This chapter describes a method of reducing the peak-to-average power ratio (PAPR) and introduces PAPR-optimal phase shifters for multicarrier communication systems.

One of the important problems inherent in multicarrier communication systems is a need to control and, ultimately, reduce the value of the PAPR. Undesirably high amplitude values of the transmitted signal are typically caused by the closeness of phases of the input components of the multitone transformation module (usually, the inverse discrete Fourier transform [IDFT]) of the transmitter. The solution to this problem should comprise a phase shifter that scrambles the data before they are converted into the transmitted broadband signal (e.g., OFDM or DMT symbol in commonly used multicarrier systems). At the receiver, a phase deshifter should be applied accordingly. Gimlin and Patisaul [1] consider the problem of phasing several equal-amplitude sinusoids and describe an optimal phase shifter that is due to Newman [2]. A similar phase shifter for a multicarrier wireless communication system is described by Carney [3]. Another possible solution was proposed by May [4], comprising an adaptive training of a communication system to reduce the PAPR. Work on developing optimized phase shifters was also performed by Jafarkhani and Tarokh [5].

Existing solutions usually comprise an "ultimate" phase shifter, i.e., a unique sequence that can be hard-coded. It is important to attain a general understanding of the structure of optimal phase shifters regardless of the specifics of the multitone transformation used. It is also important to develop an analytical foundation for easily generating such phase shifters for specific parameters of the multitone transformation.

In the following text, we describe PAPR-optimal phase shifters for multicarrier communications. A phase shifter comprises two complex, constant envelope sequences. The first is the worst-case sequence; the phases of the second are the differences between the phases of a principal shifter and those of the first sequence. A principal shifter is shown to be a complex, constant envelope sequence mapped by the multitone transformation used to another complex, constant envelope sequence. In the case of IDFT being the multitone transformation, a family of principal shifters of the form $z(r) = \exp\left(\pm j * \pi * p * \left(r^2/q\right)\right)$ has been analytically constructed, where $j^2 = -1$, $0 \le r < q$, q is the number of subcarriers, and p and q are mutually prime integers of different parity. These phase shifters outperform the best existing phase shifters by as much as 2.6 dB.

5.2 Optimal Phase Shifters and the Constant Envelope Principle

In the following description, well-known circuits, structures, and techniques have not been shown in detail in order not to unnecessarily obscure the results.

Figure 5.1 and Figure 5.2 show an outline of the multicarrier system relevant to our study. The system comprises a transmitter (Figure 5.1) and a receiver (Figure 5.2). The transmitter includes an encoder module, a phase shifter module, an IDFT module, and a front-end (RF)

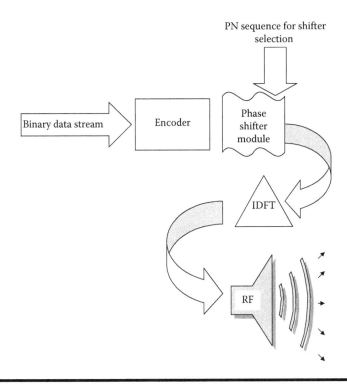

Figure 5.1   An outline of the transmitter of a multicarrier communication system.

module. The receiver includes a front-end (RF) module, a discrete Fourier transform (DFT) module, a phase deshifter module, and a decoder module. The encoder/decoder modules include at least q constellation encoders/decoders, where q is the number of subcarriers. The encoder/decoder modules may also include a channel encoder/decoder; however, this feature is irrelevant to further consideration and will not be discussed in the following text. The purpose of PN sequences in Figure 5.1 and Figure 5.2 will be explained later. Optimizing the phase shifter/deshifter modules is the main purpose of this study.

At time intervals of a predetermined duration, a block of binary data enters the encoder module at the transmitter. The output sequence of this module is a block a of symbols of the length q that are convenient to present as complex numbers with values in the range defined by the specific structure of the encoder. This sequence is an input to the multitone transformation module. The output of this module is a baseband signal to be transmitted. It enters the RF module

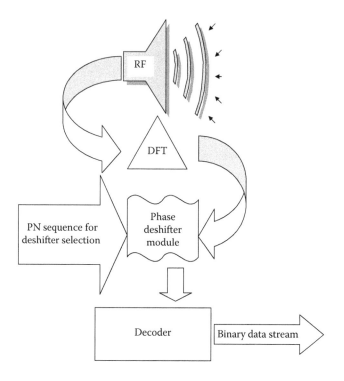

Figure 5.2   An outline of the receiver of a multicarrier communication system.

where it is up-converted and transmitted over the channel. The received signal is down-converted in the RF module, processed through the inverse multitone transformation module, deshifted, and, finally, decoded.

It can be assumed, with no loss of generality, that the multitone transformation is IDFT. The sequence a is transformed by the IDFT module as follows:

$$\vec{y} = G\vec{a}, \ G = HB$$

$$\vec{y} = \{y_n\}, \ \vec{a} = \{a_n\}, \ B = \{\delta_{nr}b_n\}, \ H = \{h_{nr}\}, \ n, r = 0, \ ..., \ q - 1 \qquad (5.2.1)$$

In Equation 5.2.1, B is a diagonal phase shifter matrix, δ_{nr} is the Kronecker symbol, H is the IDFT matrix, and **y** is the output of the IDFT module. Using Equation 5.2.1, the PAPR of the output sequence **y** is defined as follows:

$$\text{PAPR} = \frac{q \max_n |y_n|^2}{\sum_{n=0}^{q-1} |y_n|^2} = \frac{q \max_n \left| \sum_{r=0}^{q-1} h_{nr} b_r a_r \right|^2}{\sum_{n=0}^{q-1} \left| \sum_{r=0}^{q-1} h_{nr} b_r a_r \right|^2} \qquad (5.2.2)$$

A standard approach to evaluating PAPR in Equation 5.2.2 is using a worst-case data sequence $\mathbf{a} = \mathbf{x}$. Usually, this sequence is chosen such that its components are the same. As the PAPR functional in Equation 5.2.2 is homogenous with respect to a, it can be assumed, without loss of generality, that all components of $\mathbf{x}$ are 1. This choice of $\mathbf{x}$ is natural as the Fourier transform of a constant is the delta function that has the largest PAPR. This means that:

$$\vec{x} = \vec{1} \Rightarrow (\vec{1}, \vec{z}):$$

$$\text{PAPR}\left(\vec{x}, \vec{z}\right) = \min_b \text{PAPR}\left(\vec{x}, \vec{b}\right)$$

$$= \min_b \frac{q \max_n \left| \sum_{r=0}^{q-1} h_{nr} b_r x_r \right|^2}{\sum_{n=0}^{q-1} \left| \sum_{r=0}^{q-1} h_{nr} b_r x_r \right|^2} = \min_b \frac{q \max_n \left| \sum_{r=0}^{q-1} h_{nr} b_r \right|^2}{\sum_{n=0}^{q-1} \left| \sum_{r=0}^{q-1} h_{nr} b_r \right|^2} = 1 \qquad (5.2.3)$$

Equation 5.2.3 shows that PAPR is minimized, for $\mathbf{x} = \mathbf{1}$, at the sequence $\mathbf{b} = \mathbf{z}$, whose components have the same absolute value (by the definition of a shifter sequence) and whose multitone transformation has all components of the same absolute value as well. The sequence $\mathbf{z}$ is termed a *principal shifter.*

This result can be generalized by considering a wider class of worst-case sequences with components having the same absolute value but possibly different phases. It follows from Equation 5.2.3 that in order to minimize the PAPR, the product of each component of a worst-case sequence and of the corresponding shifter sequence should be equal to the corresponding component of the principal shifter sequence:

$$\left| \vec{x} \right| = 1 \Rightarrow \left(\vec{x}, \vec{b} \right) : b_r x_r = z_r, r = 0, ..., q - 1 \qquad (5.2.4)$$

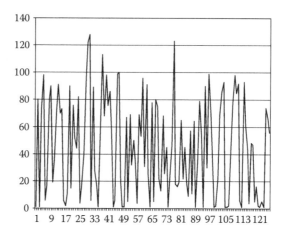

Figure 5.3 A normalized phase function f(r) of a principal shifter obtained in numerical simulations for 128-carrier system.

Again, the principal shifter is a complex sequence of constant envelope

$$\vec{z} = \left\{ \exp\left(\frac{2j\pi f(r)}{q} \right) \right\}, r = 0, \ldots, q - 1, j^2 = -1 \qquad (5.2.5)$$

mapped by the multitone transformation to another complex sequence of constant envelope. It follows from Equation 5.2.5 that the principal shifter is defined by its normalized phase f(r), a real-valued function such that $0 < f(r) \le q$.

It follows from Equation 5.2.4 that considering worst-case sequences with components having different absolute values is not reasonable because it results in different absolute values of the components of the shifter sequence which, in turn, yields variations in the signal power.

Principal shifters can be generated numerically for a given multitone transformation. Figure 5.3 shows an example of f(r) of a principal shifter for 128-IDFT computed by minimizing PAPR functional in Equation 5.2.3. The values of f(r) for this principal shifter are:

1 80 1 73 98 6 17 80 90 19 36 72 91 70 73 6 2 11 90 15 76 52 44
82 4 17 40 96 122 128 6 89 28 17 1 66 113 68 98 76 86 57 1 6 99 100
19 1 1 67 5 69 32 50 35 4 69 53 96 31 91 26 1 78 5 80 75 22 13 68
26 45 1 28 46 123 18 16 19 65 22 45 18 9 57 11 64 1 34 79 54 1 90
30 99 72 42 1 2 22 69 86 93 1 1 2 45 78 98 85 92 6 1 93 61 43 4 48
47 5 16 2 1 5 1 74 66 56

However, this method is not perfect, as it is hard to numerically attain the absolute minimum of 1 in Equation 5.2.3. Therefore, it is desirable to develop an analytical method of generating sequences that would satisfy the constant envelope property.

5.3 Flat Spectrum Chirps

In the following text, it will be proved that for q-DFT, a class of sequences satisfying the constant envelope property is given by the formula:

$$\vec{z}(r) = \left\{ \exp\left(\pm \frac{j\pi r^2 p}{q} \right) \right\}$$ (5.3.1)

In Equation 5.3.1, r varies between 0 and $q - 1$, and p and q are mutually prime and have different parities. Equation 5.3.1 describes linear chirps that are well known in digital communications. However, only chirps with p and q specified earlier would satisfy the constant envelope property for q-DFT. To show this, let us consider the following sum:

$$S(p,q) = \sum_{r=0}^{q-1} \exp\left(-\frac{j\pi r^2 p}{q} \right)$$ (5.3.2)

This is termed the *Gauss sum* and is considered in number theory (Katz [6]). The Gauss sum happens to be the sum of components of the principal shifter in Equation 5.3.1. First, it will be proved that the absolute value of a Gauss sum, for p and q specified, is independent of p. Some known properties of Gauss sums will be used. The first property is its multiplicativity:

$$\left(q', q'' \right) = 1 \implies S(p, q'q'') = S(pq', q'')S(pq'', q')$$ (5.3.3)

i.e., at mutually prime q and q, the sum on the left-hand side of Equation 5.3.3 can be presented as a product of two other sums. Apply the property (Equation 5.3.3) to the Gauss sum as follows:

$$S(1,pq) = S(p,q)\,S(q, p)$$ (5.3.4)

It did not seem to simplify the problem; however, there is another property of Gauss sums called the *Schaar's identity*, and it holds for mutually prime p and q of opposite parity. This identity can be presented as follows:

$$S^*(p, q) = \exp\left(\frac{j\pi}{4}\right)\sqrt{\frac{q}{p}}\, S(q, p) \tag{5.3.5}$$

where "*" denotes a complex conjugate. Combining Equation 5.3.4 and Equation 5.3.5 yields:

$$\exp\left(\frac{j\pi}{4}\right)\sqrt{\frac{q}{p}}\, S(1, pq) = \left|S(p, q)\right|^2 \tag{5.3.6}$$

The sum on the left-hand side of Equation 5.3.6 can be evaluated by again using the Schaar's identity:

$$S(1, pq) = \exp\left(\frac{-j\pi}{4}\right)\sqrt{pq}\, S^*(pq, 1) = \exp\left(-\frac{j\pi}{4}\right)\sqrt{pq} \tag{5.3.7}$$

Introducing Equation 5.3.7 into Equation 5.3.6 yields:

$$\left|S(p, q)\right|^2 = q \tag{5.3.8}$$

This is what had to be proved.

It turns out that the condition of p and q being mutually prime integers of opposite parity yields the required constant envelope property for the DFT of the principal shifter in Equation 5.3.1. To prove it, first notice that for p and q of opposite parity, shifting r in this Gauss sum does not change it:

$$\sum_{r=0}^{q-1}\exp\left(-\frac{j\pi r^2 p}{q}\right) = \sum_{r=0}^{q-1}\exp\left(-\frac{j\pi(r+m)^2 p}{q}\right) \tag{5.3.9}$$

The property (Equation 5.3.9) can be easily proved by induction. Now, Equation 5.3.9 is equivalent to the following equation:

$$\sum_{r=0}^{q-1} \exp\left(-\frac{2j\pi nr}{q} - \frac{j\pi r^2 p}{q}\right) = S(p, q) \exp\left(\frac{j\pi m^2 p}{q}\right), \tag{5.3.10}$$

$$mp = n \ (\text{mod } q)$$

Equation 5.3.10 establishes a relation between the DFT of a chirp with parameters p and q specified earlier and the Gauss sum in Equation 5.3.2. As p and q are mutually prime, it is always possible, for a given n, to find m such that remainders of dividing mp and n by q are equal. Moreover, for a given n, such m is uniquely found. Therefore, the DFT of such a chirp has a constant envelope equal to the absolute value of the corresponding Gauss sum:

$$\left|\sum_{r=0}^{q-1} \exp\left(-\frac{2j\pi nr}{q} - \frac{j\pi r^2 p}{q}\right)\right| = |S(p, q)| = \sqrt{q} \tag{5.3.11}$$

A chirp whose constant envelope property pertains to the DFT is termed the *flat spectrum chirp* (FSC). Although the proof was presented for FSC with the minus sign in Equation 5.3.1, because absolute values of a complex number and its conjugate are equal, the constant envelope property holds for FSC with the plus sign as well in Equation 5.3.1. Also, as the IDFT matrix is, up to a constant multiplier 1/q, a conjugate to the DFT matrix, the constant envelope property for FSC in Equation 5.3.1 pertains to IDFT as well.

Figure 5.4 and Figure 5.5 show examples of f(r) of FSC at q = 64 and p = 5 and 1, respectively. These functions are symmetrical with respect to the middle of the interval (0, q). Figure 5.6 to Figure 5.8 show the dependence of the envelope variance of the DFT of chirps on p/2 at q = 4, 16, and 64, respectively. These figures present a numerical corroboration of the constant envelope property of FSC. They show that the variance vanishes at p/2 = 0.5 + s, where s is an integer. For practical applications, the case of q being a power of 2 is the most important one because then the FFT can be used for the DFT. In this case, FSC corresponds to p being an odd integer. Figure 5.9 shows the dependence of the envelope variance of the DFT of chirps on p/2 at q = 9. As follows from the theory presented in the preceding text, the variance should vanish at p = 2, 4, and 8; Figure 5.9 shows that it does. Figure 5.10 and Figure 5.11 show a distribution of values of components of FSC and of the DFT of FSC, respectively,

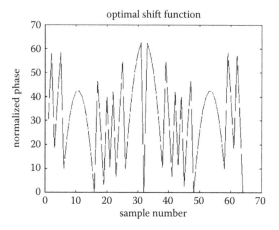

Figure 5.4 **f(r) of a flat spectrum chirp at q = 64 and p = 61.**

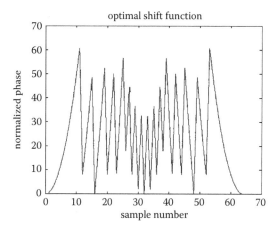

Figure 5.5 **f(r) of a flat spectrum chirp at q = 64 and p = 1.**

at $q = 64$; the constant envelope property holds. If q is an odd prime number, an appropriate set of FSC corresponds to $p = 2s$, where $s = 1, \ldots, q - 1$. At $q = 61$, a distribution of values of components of DFT of FSC is shown in Figure 5.12; the constant envelope property holds. Figure 5.13 and Figure 5.14 show these distributions in cases when some of the conditions used in deriving the constant envelope property of FSC are violated. Figure 5.13 corresponds to the set of FSC shown in Figure 5.12 appended by one more chirp with $p = q$. The distribution now contains two additional points that do not lie on the circle. Figure

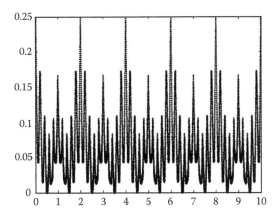

Figure 5.6 **The p/2 dependence of the variance of the amplitude of discrete Fourier transform (DFT) of a chirp at q = 4.**

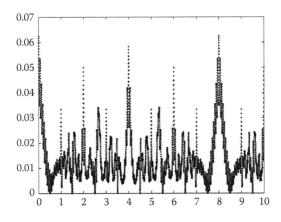

Figure 5.7 **The p/2 dependence of the variance of the amplitude of DFT of a chirp at q = 16.**

5.14 corresponds to q = 61 and positive p smaller than q. The values of components of the DFT of these chirps are spread all over the complex plane. Although, in this set, p are mutually prime to q, the second condition that should be imposed on p is violated because some p are of the same parity as q.

If FSCs are used as phase shifters, the worst-case sequence consisting of identical components becomes an optimal input sequence to the phase shifter module corresponding to the PAPR of unity, regardless of a specific FSC. Moreover, in cases of q being a prime

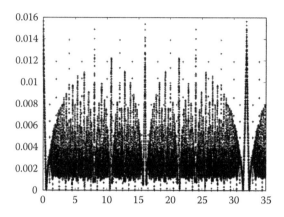

Figure 5.8 The p/2 dependence of the variance of the amplitude of DFT of a chirp at q = 64.

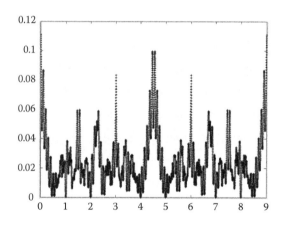

Figure 5.9 The p/2 dependence of the variance of the amplitude of DFT of a chirp at q = 9.

number or a power of 2, one can construct a plurality of such optimal input sequences. Specifically, choosing an arbitrary pair of FSC, components of an optimal input sequence are ratios of corresponding components of the first to the second FSC. These optimal input sequences can be employed as signaling patterns in communication protocols used for multicarrier systems.

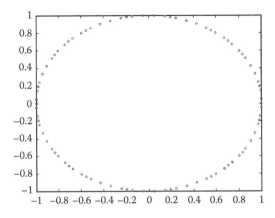

Figure 5.10 **A distribution of components of FSC on the complex plane at q = 64.**

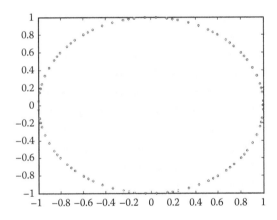

Figure 5.11 **A distribution of components of DFT of FSC on the complex plane at q = 64.**

5.4 Simulations of Multicarrier Transmission

A Matlab simulator was developed to verify the effectiveness of the phase shifters introduced in the preceding text. Figure 5.15 to Figure 5.28 present the results of simulations. An orthogonal frequency division multiplexing (OFDM) transmission system was simulated. The total number of subcarriers was 64. For each subcarrier, a 64-QAM

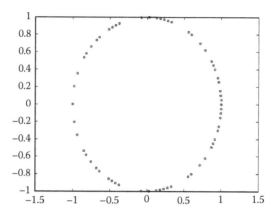

Figure 5.12   A distribution of components of DFT of FSC on the complex plane at q = 61 and at p = 2m, m = 1, ..., 60.

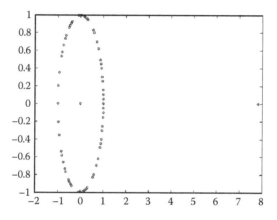

Figure 5.13   A distribution of components of DFT of a chirp on the complex plane at q = 61 and at p = 2m, m = 1, ..., 61.

constellation encoder was used. A baseband *additive white Gaussian noise* (AWGN) channel with signal-to-noise ratio (SNR) of 40 dB was considered. Eight sets of OFDM symbols were transmitted. Each set consisted of 100 OFDM symbols. Sets with larger-order numbers had been formed out of more inhomogeneous data. Figure 5.15 to Figure 5.17 are examples of IDFT input sequences corresponding to different sets. For sets with larger order numbers, components of input sequences are increasingly localized in the fourth quadrant of the complex plane.

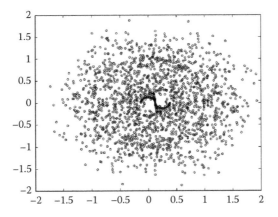

Figure 5.14 A distribution of components of DFT of a chirp on the complex plane at q = 61 and at p = m, m = 1, ..., 60.

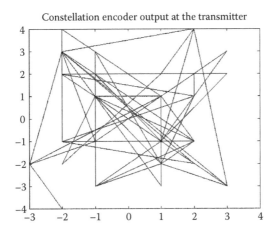

Figure 5.15 An example of the constellation encoder module output at the transmitter of a 64-carrier system simulated.

For phase shifters, (p,64)-FSC were used. For a given IDFT input sequence, p was chosen as a successive element of a predefined, generally pseudorandom sequence of odd integers; this is illustrated in Figure 5.1 and Figure 5.2. The worst-case sequence was chosen with all components equal to unity. Figure 5.18 shows a comparison between the PAPR averaged over each set of OFDM symbols, with phase shifters applied (circles) and without (diamonds), for different

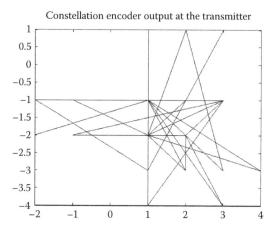

Figure 5.16   An example of the constellation encoder module output at the transmitter of a 64-carrier system simulated, for the third most homogeneous dataset.

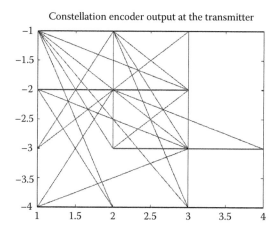

Figure 5.17   An example of the constellation encoder module output at the transmitter of a 64-carrier system simulated, for the most inhomogeneous dataset.

sets. The phase shifters proposed act more and more effectively as the inhomogeneity of the input data increases. For the most asymmetric dataset (the last one), using phase shifters yields approximately a 20-fold decrease in PAPR.

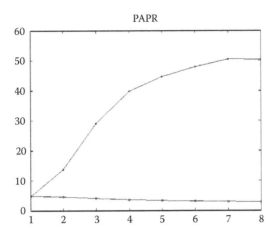

Figure 5.18 A comparison between PAPR averaged over datasets of different homogeneity with phase shifters (circles) and without (diamonds).

Figure 5.19 shows the distribution of components of a transmitted OFDM symbol on the complex plane, in the case of the most asymmetric dataset, without phase shifters applied. One of the components is way off the area of the plane in which the rest are localized, which results in a high PAPR value. Figure 5.20 shows the corresponding data at the output of a DFT module at the receiver. Figure 5.21 shows the distribution of components of the transmitted OFDM symbol on the complex plane for the same input data that were used in Figure 5.19. This figure presents the results with phase shifters applied; unlike Figure 5.19, this distribution of components is compact. Figure 5.22 shows the corresponding data at the output of the DFT module at the receiver. Figure 5.20 and Figure 5.22 look identical; this means that applying phase shifters greatly reduces PAPR without negatively affecting the system performance. The figure showing the output of the constellation decoder module is not presented as it is identical to Figure 5.17. In all simulations performed at the SNR of 40 dB, no transmission errors were observed. Figure 5.23 shows the mean square deviation of PAPR over OFDM symbols from the same set, for different sets, in the case of phase shifters applied. The PAPR variation is largest in the case of the most homogeneous set and smallest in that of the most inhomogeneous set. Figure 5.24 shows the mean square deviation of PAPR over OFDM symbols from the same set, for different sets, in the case of no phase shifters. As in Figure 5.23, the PAPR variation is largest in the case of the most homogeneous set, and it is smallest for

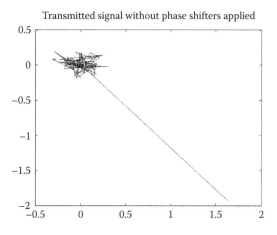

Figure 5.19   A distribution on the complex plane of components of an OFDM symbol transmitted, in the case of the most asymmetric (the last one) dataset, without phase shifters applied.

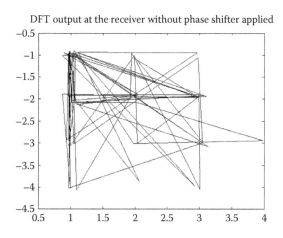

Figure 5.20   A distribution on the complex plane of components of a data sequence at the output of DFT module at the receiver, in the case of the most asymmetric (the last one) dataset, without phase shifters applied.

the most inhomogeneous set. However, comparing Figure 5.23 and Figure 5.24 shows that although in the most homogeneous and inhomogeneous cases the mean square deviation without phase shifters is about the same as with phase shifters, for sets of intermediate homogeneity the mean square deviation without phase shifters is as much

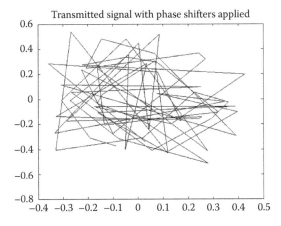

Figure 5.21 A distribution on the complex plane of components of an OFDM symbol transmitted, in the case of the most asymmetric (the last one) dataset, with phase shifters applied.

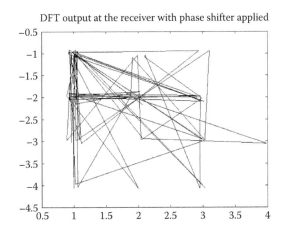

Figure 5.22 A distribution on the complex plane of components of a data sequence at the output of DFT module at the receiver, in the case of the most asymmetric (the last one) dataset, with phase shifters applied.

as six times higher than that with phase shifters. Therefore, applying the proposed phase shifters greatly reduces both instantaneous and average PAPR.

Figure 5.25 to Figure 5.28 present results of simulations of a system with the total number of subcarriers not being equal to a power of 2.

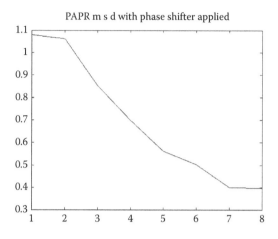

Figure 5.23 **The mean square deviation of PAPR over OFDM symbols from the same set, for different sets, in case of phase shifters applied.**

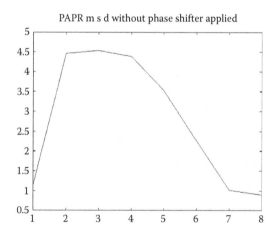

Figure 5.24 **The mean square deviation of PAPR over OFDM symbols from the same set, for different sets, in case of no phase shifters.**

In all these cases, 4-QAM constellation encoders were used to simulate the constellation encoder module. This means that OFDM symbols were sums of harmonic waves of the same amplitude. Figure 5.25 shows PAPR averaged over datasets of different homogeneity, for a chirp with p = 1 as a phase shifter, in a 61-carrier communication system. The existing results (Gimlin and Patisaul [1]; Shlien [7]) suggest

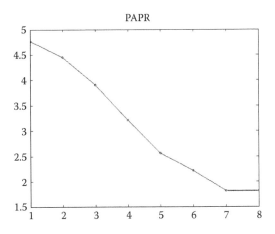

Figure 5.25 The PAPR averaged over datasets of different homogeneity, for a chirp with p = 1 as a phase shifter, in a 61-carrier communication system.

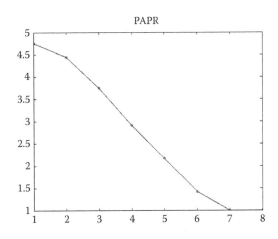

Figure 5.26 The PAPR averaged over datasets of different homogeneity, for an FSC with p = 20 as a phase shifter, in a 61-carrier communication system.

that this phase shifter is the best possible that should yield PAPR of 2.6 dB in the most inhomogeneous dataset. This number is confirmed in simulations that yield PAPR of 1.8, which converts into approximately 2.6 dB. However, the results presented in this chapter suggest that this phase shifter is not optimal; at q = 61, the optimal shifters correspond to even positive p smaller than 122. Figure 5.26 shows PAPR for an FSC with p = 20 as a phase shifter in the same system. Comparing

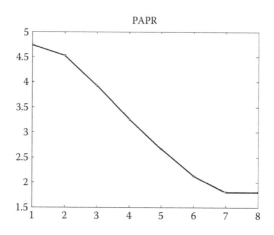

Figure 5.27 **The PAPR averaged over datasets of different homogeneity, for a chirp with p = 1 as a phase shifter, in a 63-carrier communication system.**

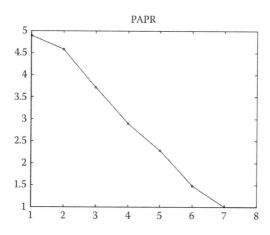

Figure 5.28 **The PAPR averaged over datasets of different homogeneity, for an FSC with p = 2 as a phase shifter, in a 63-carrier communication system.**

these figures shows that this phase shifter outperforms the best conventional one by 2.6 dB in the most inhomogeneous dataset yielding PAPR of unity. Figure 5.27 shows PAPR averaged over datasets of different homogeneity, for a chirp with p = 1 as a phase shifter, in a 63-channel communication system. Figure 5.28 shows PAPR for an FSC with p = 2 as a phase shifter in the same system. Again, the proposed phase shifter outperforms the best conventional one by as much as 2.6 dB.

5.5 Possible Applications of FSC

The proposed FSC are excellent phase shifters that yield a significant reduction in PAPR. There is additional benefit in using multiple FSC instead of just one. In a large network, each node can be assigned a pseudorandom sequence of integers. A node may have a unique sequence assigned to its links, or it may have separate sequences for separate links. Information about these sequences is exchanged between peers at the beginning of a communication session. At each node subsequent output sequences of the encoder are phase-shifted with a (p,q)-FSC where p equals a current value from the sequence. Such phase shifters protect the communication security of a link on the physical layer. As they are equivalent performance-wise, combining them does not affect the performance of the system negatively.

Another potential application of FSC is to protect privileged information PAPR-wise. Some information may be so valuable that the data rate is unimportant in comparison to the absence of transmission errors. In these circumstances, clipping peaks of a signal generated at the transmitter is unacceptable. This can be avoided by temporarily assigning all subcarriers for these data. As a result, each sequence at the output of the encoder module will have identical components, whereas the information may vary between different sequences. Applying FSC to each of these sequences guarantees that the transmission of the privileged data will have a PAPR of unity.

5.6 Conclusions

In this chapter, we introduced a method of selecting an optimal phase shifter for reducing PAPR and for data transmission in a general multicarrier communication system employing this phase shifter. Such a multicarrier communication system comprises a transmitter and a receiver, including the following:

An encoder module of the transmitter
A phase shifter module of the transmitter
A multitone transformation module of the transmitter
A transmitter front-end module
A receiver front-end module
An inverse multitone transformation module of the receiver
A phase deshifter module of the receiver
A decoder module of the receiver

The multicarrier communication system includes q subcarriers, the encoder module includes q constellation encoders, the decoder module includes q constellation decoders, the multitone transformation is the q-point IDFT, and the inverse multitone transformation is the q-point DFT.

Selecting an optimal phase shifter comprises selecting a worst-case sequence and a phase shifter sequence. The worst-case sequence and phase shifter sequence are complex, constant envelope data sequences of the length q. The phases of this phase shifter sequence are the differences between the phases of a principal shifter and those of the worst-case sequence. The principal shifter is a complex, constant envelope data sequence mapped by the multitone transformation to another complex, constant envelope data sequence.

The main result of this chapter is introducing a new class of principal shifters, FSC, of the form:

$$ z(r) = \exp\left(\pm\frac{j\pi p r^2}{q}\right) $$

where $j^2 = -1$, r is an integer such that $0 \le r < q$, and p and q are mutually prime integers of different parity.

The method of data transmission in a multicarrier communication system using these FSC comprises (at each time interval of a predetermined duration) processing a block of binary data of a predetermined length through the encoder module, multiplying components of an output sequence of the encoder module by components of the phase shifter sequence, processing the output of the phase shifter module through the multitone transformation module and computing a broadband signal, up-converting and transmitting the broadband signal using the transmitter front-end module, receiving and down-converting the broadband signal using the receiver front-end module, processing an output of the receiver front-end module through the inverse multitone transformation module, dividing components of an output sequence of the inverse multitone transformation module by components of the phase shifter sequence, and processing an output of the phase deshifter module through the decoder module and retrieving the block of binary data at the receiver.

These FSC can provide a mechanism of enhancing the security of communications in the physical layer by storing identical copies of a pseudorandom sequence at the transmitter and at the receiver, determining a current element of the pseudorandom sequence at the transmitter, selecting a phase shifter sequence at the transmitter based on the value of this element, determining a current element of the pseudorandom sequence at the receiver, and selecting a phase shifter sequence at the receiver based on the value of this element. This mechanism implies a correspondence between elements of the pseudorandom sequence and FSC with parameters p and q such that different elements of the pseudorandom sequence correspond to different values of p. In a network, employing such a mechanism would enhance the security of multicarrier communications, provided that this pseudorandom sequence is protected from unauthorized access.

Another application of FSC would be controlling the PAPR in transmitting a privileged data by temporarily assigning all subcarriers for the privileged data such that the broadband signal corresponding to the privileged data has a PAPR of unity.

Finally, if q is either a prime number or a power of 2, a communication system employing FSC as phase shifters has a set of PAPR-optimal input sequences that can be used as signaling patterns. The broadband signal corresponding to such a sequence has the PAPR of unity. The r-th element of such a sequence can be computed by selecting any two FSC and, for each integer r such that $0 \leq r < q$, computing a ratio of the r-th component of the first to the second of the selected FSC.

References

1. Gimlin, D.R., Patisaul, C.R., On minimizing the peak-to-average power ratio for the sum of N sinusoids, *IEEE Trans. Commun.*, Vol. 41, No. 4, 631–635, April 1993.
2. Newman, D.J., An L1 extremal problem for polynomials, *Proc. Am. Math. Soc.*, Vol. 16, p. 1287-1290, December 1965.
3. Carney, R.R., Reducing Peak-to-Average Variance of a Composite Transmitted Signal Generated by a Digital Combiner via Carrier Phase Offset, U.S. Patent No. 5,838,732 A, November 17, 1998.
4. May, M.R., Johnson, T.L., and Pendleton, M.A., Method and Apparatus for Reducing Peak-to-Average Requirements in Multi-Tone Communication Circuits, U.S. Patent No. 5,835,536 A, November 10, 1998.
5. Jafarkhani, H., Tarokh, V., Method and Apparatus to Reduce Peak to Average Power Ratio in Multi-Carrier Modulation, U.S. Patent No. US 6,445,747 B1, September 3, 2002.
6. Katz, N.M., *Gauss Sums, Kloosterman Sums, and Monodromy Groups*, Princeton, NJ: Princeton University Press, 1987.

7. Shlien, S., Minimization of the peak amplitude of a waveform, *Signal Process.*, Vol. 14, 91–93, 1998.
8. Proakis, J.G., *Digital Communications*, McGraw-Hill, New York, 1995.
9. Mitlin, V., Phase Shifters for Peak-to-Average Power Ratio Reduction for Multicarrier Communications, U.S. Patent Application No. 10/945,974, pending.

Chapter 6

Optimization of the Automatic Repeat Request Parameters in Quadrature Amplitude Modulation Channels

6.1 Background

Broadband and high-quality wireless communication systems have been standardized recently in the European Telecommunications Standards Institute (ETSI) Broadband Radio Access Network (BRAN) [1] and IEEE 802.16 [2]. To realize high-quality broadband wireless communications, the use of automatic repeat request (ARQ) in combination with forward error correction (FEC) is being considered. In wireless communications, if there are some obstructions interfering with the signal transmitted, consecutive frame errors (burst errors) occur. Thus, ARQ is especially required. Several ARQ schemes have been proposed and introduced in actual wireless communication systems [3–5]. At the same time, in wireline communication systems such as Asymmetrical Digital Subscriber Line (ADSL) [6], ARQ is currently considered for inclusion in the International Telecommunications Union (ITU) standard [7].

The purpose of this chapter is to present a general methodology for optimal selection of ARQ parameters. The chapter is structured as follows. First, for an *additive white Gaussian noise* (AWGN) quadrature amplitude modulation (QAM) channel with FEC and ARQ, the bit error rate (BER) is estimated as a function of the channel signal-to-noise ratio (SNR). A method of trading off the maximum allowed number of transmissions k and the margin applied to the channel SNR is presented. Particularly, a channel without ARQ characterized by some margin is equivalent (BER-wise) to a channel with ARQ and with a lower margin. An explicit relationship between the increase in k and the margin decrease (or the line ARQ gain) is derived. A systematic procedure of simultaneously adjusting the bit load, FEC and ARQ parameters, and throughput in the channel initialization procedure is proposed.

We introduce and discuss the distinction between the line ARQ gain and the net ARQ gain, the first related to the total increase in data transmission and used in the bit loading, the second discounted for FEC redundancy and retransmissions. Unlike the line ARQ gain, which typically grows monotonically with increasing k, the net ARQ gain attains a maximum at certain k_{opt} (the optimum allowable number of transmissions). Then we prove the central result of this chapter, i.e., the line ARQ gain maximizing the channel throughput is a sum of the channel SNR and some function of the bit load and FEC parameters. Based on this result, we formulate an efficient method of determining the optimum ARQ parameters at the actual channel conditions, given their values at some reference conditions, the latter being either stored in the modem memory or calculated prior to channel initialization. Derivations for a slowly fading channel are presented at the end of the chapter.

6.2 Derivation of the BER of a QAM Channel with FEC and ARQ

Consider a data transmission between two stations in an AWGN QAM channel. The error-controlling algorithm uses a combination of an FEC code and a cyclic redundancy check (CRC). The FEC can be any type of code but here we will consider the Reed–Solomon (RS) code as an outer code and a convolutional code as an inner code.

A binary convolutional code with a soft-decision decoder having the minimum free distance of d* and the rate of h/H is considered. For our purposes, one has to introduce weighting coefficients $\{\beta_d\}$ of the code obtained by expanding the first derivative of its transfer function [8].

Each information frame of the RS code has a length of N code symbols containing an information field of length K symbols. The N − K redundant code symbols are divided into a CRC field of length C symbols and a parity check field of length R symbols, i.e., N = K + C + R. Generally, the number of correctable symbol errors, t, can be determined from R as follows. If e_r positions of supposedly unreliable code symbols (erasures) are made known to the decoder, then the number of errors that can be corrected by an RS code with redundancy R is

$$t = \left\lfloor \frac{R + 1 + e_r}{2} \right\rfloor,$$

where the maximum of errors corrected by correctly identifying erasures is R, and this is reached when e_r = R. In case of no erasures and at even R, t = R/2.

The FEC is assumed to correct all information frames that are received with no more than t errors. Also, for any frame with more than t errors, the CRC is assumed to always detect the residual errors after FEC. In this case, a negative acknowledgment frame will be sent to the peer, and the frame will be retransmitted. A limit of k is imposed on the number of frame transmissions (k = 1 indicates that no retransmissions will take place). Each acknowledgment frame is assumed to be much shorter than N. Our other simplifying assumptions are that no packets are lost in transmission and that all acknowledgment frames are received correctly.

The probability p of an RS frame being accepted by this scheme is described by the following pair of equations [8,9]:

$$p = \sum_{i=0}^{t} p_e^i (1 - p_e)^{N-i} \binom{N}{i}$$

$$1 - (1 - p_e)^{1/\alpha} = \frac{1}{h} \sum_{d=d^*}^{d-1} \beta_d \, p_b^d \sum_{m=0}^{d-1} (1 - p_b)^m \binom{d-1+m}{m} \quad (6.2.1)$$

Here, p_e is the RS symbol error rate after the inner (convolutional) but before the outer (RS) decoder, p_b is the bit error rate before the inner decoder, and α is the number of bits per RS symbol. At small p_e, the probability of a frame being erroneously decoded after one transmission can be approximated by $1 - p$ ([9], p. 465; [10], p. 19; [11], p. 269).

The fraction of erroneous RS symbols in the output stream, *symbol error rate* (SER), after all detection, correction, and retransmission work is done, can be estimated using Equation 6.2.1. A frame at the receiver contains errors only if it has not passed through FEC and CRC after k transmissions. If such a frame has i > t errors, it will be in the output stream with probability:

$$q_i = (1 - p)^{k-1} p_e^i (1 - p_e)^{N-1} \binom{N}{i}$$

i.e., more than t errors were found in the frame in each of the first k − 1 transmissions, and i > t errors were found after the k-th transmission. Thus the SER will be:

$$SER = \frac{1}{N} \sum_{i=t+1}^{N} i q_i$$

$$= \left[\sum_{i=t+1}^{N} p_e^i (1 - p_e)^{N-i} \binom{N-1}{i-1} \right] \left[\sum_{i=t+1}^{N} p_e^i (1 - p_e)^{N-i} \binom{N}{i} \right]^{k-1}$$

$$(6.2.2)$$

Another useful parameter is the average number of transmissions, v, needed for a frame to get to the output stream. It can be expressed in the following form:

$$v = 1 \cdot p + 2 \cdot p (1 - p) + ... + k \cdot p (1 - p)^{k-1} + k \cdot (1 - p)^k$$

$$= \frac{1 - (1 - p)^k}{p}$$

$$(6.2.3)$$

i.e., a frame is either good after the FEC at the first, or the second, or the (k − 1)-th transmission, or it is found noncorrectable at the k-th transmission and is still passed to the output stream.

If ε is the BER level at the output after FEC and ARQ, then the SER level, ε_s, can be approximated as follows ([7], p. 256; [11], p. 269):

$$\varepsilon_S = 1 - (1 - \varepsilon)^\alpha \approx \alpha\varepsilon, \text{ as } \varepsilon \ll 1 \qquad (6.2.4)$$

Equation 6.2.4 means that a decoded RS symbol is not in error when all its α bits are error-free. The approximation made in Equation 6.2.4 uses the linear term of the Taylor expansion of a function at small values of its argument. The SER determined in Equation 6.2.2 ultimately depends on the channel bit error rate, p_b. For $\varepsilon_s \ll 1$, this dependency can be inverted, i.e., p_b can be presented in the form of a function of SER after FEC and ARQ (see Section 6.7). Using Equation 6.2.4, this yields the bit error rate before FEC and ARQ, p_b, as follows:

$$p_b = \left(\frac{Wh}{\alpha\beta_{d^*}} \, \varepsilon_S^{\frac{1}{(t+1)k}} \right)^{\frac{1}{d^*}} \qquad (6.2.5)$$

where

$$W = \left[\frac{\Gamma(K+C+R)}{\Gamma(K+C+R-t)\Gamma(t+1)} \right]^{-\frac{1}{k(t+1)}} \left[\frac{\Gamma(K+C+R+1)}{\Gamma(K+C+R-t)\Gamma(t+2)} \right]^{-\frac{(k-1)}{k(t+1)}} \qquad (6.2.6)$$

where Γ is the gamma function. On the other hand, the bit error rate p_b can be approximated as follows (see [9], pp. 273 and 280):

$$p_b = \omega(b) p_{QAM},$$

$$p_{QAM} = \left(1 - 2^{-b/2}\right) \text{erfc}\left(\sqrt{3 \cdot 10^{\gamma/10} / \left(2^{b+1} - 2\right)} \right) \qquad (6.2.7)$$

$$\left[2 - \left(1 - 2^{-b/2}\right) \text{erfc}\left(\sqrt{3 \cdot 10^{\gamma/10} / \left(2^{b+1} - 2\right)} \right) \right]$$

In Equation 6.2.7, $\omega(b)$ is an average fraction of erroneous bits in an erroneous b-sized QAM symbol (see Section 6.8 and Chapter 8 for more details), γ is the channel SNR in dB, and p_{QAM} is the QAM symbol error rate. Relation between p_b and p_{QAM} is a commonly used "nearest neighbor" approximation (see [9], pp. 273, 280, and 441).

The expression for p_{QAM} in Equation 6.2.7 is exact at even values of b, and it provides a tight estimate of p_{QAM} at odd values of b. But p_b defined in Equation 6.2.7 should be equal to p_b in Equation 6.2.5, which yields the following expression for ε:

$$\varepsilon = \frac{1}{\alpha}\left[\frac{\beta_{d^*}\,\alpha}{Wh}\left(\omega(b)p_{QAM}\right)^{d^*}\right]^{(t+1)k} \tag{6.2.8}$$

or

$$\varepsilon = \frac{1}{\alpha}\left[\frac{\beta_{d^*}\alpha}{Wh}\left(\omega(b)\left(1 - 2^{\frac{-b}{2}}\right)erfc\left(\sqrt{3{\cdot}10^{\gamma/10}/2^{b+1}-2}\right) \atop \times\left(2 - \left(1-2^{-b/2}\right)erfc\left(\sqrt{3{\cdot}10^{\gamma/10}/\left(2^{b+1}-2\right)}\right)\right)\right)^{d^*}\right]^{(t+1)k} \tag{6.2.9}$$

Equation 6.2.9 relates the BER in the channel output (after FEC and ARQ) to the bit load, SNR, and FEC and ARQ parameters. Introducing the BER exponent as $\chi = -\ln \varepsilon$ and using Equation 6.2.6 yields:

$$\chi = \ln \alpha \, - \, \ln\left[\frac{\Gamma\left(K+C+R\right)}{\Gamma\left(K+C+R-t\right)\Gamma(t+1)}\right]$$

$$- \left(k-1\right)\ln\left[\frac{\Gamma\left(K+C+R+1\right)}{\Gamma\left(K+C+R-t\right)\Gamma(t+2)}\right] \tag{6.2.10}$$

$$- \left(t+1\right)k\,\ln\frac{\alpha\beta_{d^*}}{h} - d^*(t+1)k\,\ln\left[\omega(b)\,p_{QAM}\right]$$

For large SNR, using the asymptotic properties of erfc(…),

$$erfc(x) = \frac{1}{\sqrt{\pi}}\frac{\exp{(x^{-2})}}{x}\left[1+O\,(x^{-2})\right], \text{ as } x \to \infty \tag{6.2.11}$$

yields

$$\chi = \frac{1.5\left(t+1\right)kd^*{\cdot}10^{\gamma/10}}{2^b-1}\left[1+O\left(\frac{\gamma}{10^{\gamma/10}}\right)\right] \tag{6.2.12}$$

Equation 6.2.12 shows that the BER dependence on SNR in dB is quite strong (double exponent) and that doubling the number of control symbols is approximately equivalent (BER-wise) to doubling k. Equation 6.2.12 allows one to access the sensitivity of BER measurements to SNR measurement error, as follows:

$$\frac{\Delta\chi}{\chi} = 0.1 \cdot \ln 10 \cdot \Delta\gamma \qquad (6.2.13)$$

Finally, it should be mentioned that derivations of this section (e.g., approximations: Equation 6.2.1, Equation 6.2.4, and Equation 6.2.7) assume that $\varepsilon \ll 1$.

6.3 ARQ Performance Gain

Consider the following two states of the channel described. In both states, the bit loads are identical at the same BER. In the first state, both FEC and k_1-ARQ are applied, and the channel SNR is $\gamma_1 = \gamma$. In the second state, both FEC and k_2-ARQ are applied, and the channel SNR is $\gamma_2 = \gamma - \mu_1$. Equating expressions for BER derived in the preceding text for these two states yields the following equation for the line ARQ gain μ_l:

$$\frac{k_2}{k_1} = \frac{1 + \Theta(\gamma)}{1 + \Theta(\gamma - \mu_1)} \qquad (6.3.1)$$

where the function appearing in the numerator and denominator on the right-hand side of Equation 6.3.1 is defined as:

$$\Theta(\gamma) = \frac{(t+1)\ln\dfrac{\alpha\beta_{d^*}}{h} + d^*(t+1)\ln\left[\omega(b)_{P_{QAM}}\right]}{\ln\left[\dfrac{\Gamma(K+C+R+1)}{\Gamma(K+C+R-t)\Gamma(t+2)}\right]} \qquad (6.3.2)$$

For given b and FEC parameters, at large γ, one can simplify Equation 6.3.1:

$$\frac{k_2}{k_1} \approx \frac{\Theta(\gamma)}{\Theta(\gamma - \mu_1)} \approx \frac{10^{\gamma/10}}{10^{(\gamma-\mu_1)/10}} = 10^{\mu_1/10}$$

(here the asymptotic properties of erfc(...) were used), which yields:

$$\mu_1 = 10 \log\left(\frac{k_2}{k_1}\right)$$ (6.3.3)

Equation 6.3.3 shows that the larger the initially allowed number of transmissions, the less significant is the line ARQ gain attained by further increase in k.

Equations presented in this section so far describe the line ARQ gain discounted neither for the control symbols transmitted with each codeword nor for the throughput loss due to retransmissions. The net gain relevant to the change in throughput due to retransmissions is

$$\mu_n = \mu_1 + 10 \log\left(\frac{v_1}{v_2}\right)$$ (6.3.4)

where v is the average number of transmissions in channels with ARQ evaluated in Section 6.7 and given by Equation 6.7.10. In the following text, Equation 6.3.4 is derived.

Let us introduce SNR per b information bits received, γ_{i*} (as though a QAM symbol would consist of information bits only),

$$10^{\gamma_{i*}/10} = \frac{N_i v_i}{K_i} \, 10^{\gamma_i/10}, i = 1,2$$ (6.3.5)

where N_i and K_i are the total FEC frame length and the length of the information part, respectively. This yields:

$$\mu_n = \gamma_{1*} - \gamma_{2*} = 10 \log\left(\frac{\dfrac{N_1 v_1}{K_1} 10^{\gamma_1/10}}{\dfrac{N_2 v_2}{K_2} 10^{\gamma_2/10}}\right)$$ (6.3.6)

$$= \gamma_1 - \gamma_2 + 10 \log\left(\frac{N_1 K_2 v_1}{N_2 K_1 v_2}\right)$$

In our case, as the FEC parameters are the same in both states, using the line gain definition,

$$\gamma_1 - \gamma_2 = \mu_1 \qquad\qquad (6.3.7)$$

yields Equation 6.3.4.

In the particular case of $k_1 = 1$ and $k_2 = k$, instead of Equation 6.3.1, Equation 6.3.3, and Equation 6.3.4 we obtain the following equations:

$$k = \frac{1 + \Theta(\gamma)}{1 + \Theta(\gamma - \mu_1)} \qquad\qquad (6.3.8)$$

$$\mu_1 = 10 \log k \qquad\qquad (6.3.9)$$

$$\mu_n = \mu_1 - 10 \log v \qquad\qquad (6.3.10)$$

One can see from Equation 6.3.9 that at large SNR at $k = 2$, one can gain 3 dB if ARQ is applied. Also, at large γ, the performance gain in the hybrid FEC/ARQ scheme is primarily determined by ARQ, whereas at lower γ, the FEC mechanism (terms omitted in the asymptotic form [Equation 6.3.9]) contributes increasingly. Equation 6.3.9 shows that to double μ_1 at large γ, the quantity k has to be changed to k^2.

As the net ARQ gain represents the decrease in energy needed to successfully transmit b information bits, $\mu_n/10\log 2$ is an estimate for the additional (to b bits) number of information bits one can transmit at the same BER. Here, the factor $10 \log 2$ is the usual scaling factor between representations of gain in dB and bits for QAM channels. Accordingly,

$$\frac{\mu_n}{10b \log 2} \qquad\qquad (6.3.11)$$

is the relative channel throughput increase due to ARQ. Equation 6.3.11 is an approximate form for the high-order modulations.

6.4 A Method of Estimating the ARQ Gain

Let the data in a QAM channel be transmitted with the ARQ level k_1. To protect the channel from burst errors, a service provider might want to increase the ARQ level to $k_2 > k_1$. At the same time, the provider has to know whether this action would yield a better performance of the channel, i.e., whether increasing the maximum number of transmissions would yield a positive net ARQ gain (that can be used to load and transmit additional bits). To find this out, one has to subsequently estimate $k(i)$ from Equation 6.3.1 and $\mu_n(i)$ from Equation 6.3.4, given $k(i - 1)$ and $\mu_l(i - 1) = (i - 1) \times \Delta\mu_l$, where $\Delta\mu_l$ is the required precision of determining the ARQ gain (a typical $\Delta\mu_l$ value would be 0.5 dB). The initial conditions are $k(1) = k_1$ and $\mu_l(1) = \mu_n(1) = 0$. After each step, it is checked whether $\mu_n(i) > \mu_n(i - 1)$; otherwise, the calculations are stopped, as it is seen that the μ_n maximum has been reached and that raising the ARQ level to $k = k_2$ is not beneficial anymore.

For a certain i, one has $k(i - 1) \le k_2 \le k(i)$. Then, the μ_l value corresponding to $k = k_2$ can be found approximately from the following equality:

$$\frac{\mu_l - \mu_l(i)}{k - k(i)} = \frac{\mu_l - \mu_l(i - 1)}{k - k(i - 1)} \tag{6.4.1}$$

which is the first iteration of the bisection method for the equation $k(\mu_l) = k_2$. Equation 6.4.1 yields:

$$\mu_l = \frac{\left[\dfrac{\mu_l(i)}{k - k(i)} - \dfrac{\mu_l(i - 1)}{k - k(i - 1)}\right]}{\left[\dfrac{1}{k - k(i)} - \dfrac{1}{k - k(i - 1)}\right]} \tag{6.4.2}$$

The line ARQ gain determined by Equation 6.4.2 can be used for loading more bits into the channel, according to the formula:

$$\Delta b = \frac{\mu_1}{10 \log 2} \tag{6.4.3}$$

The procedure described in the preceding text has to be performed during the transceiver initialization. Figure 6.1 and Figure 6.2 illustrate this procedure. Calculations were performed in MatLab.

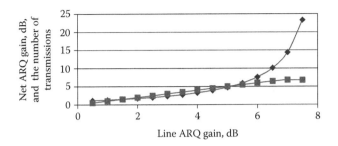

Figure 6.1 **Net ARQ gain (squares) and the number of transmissions (diamonds) versus the line ARQ gain at b = 3 bits, N = 60, R = 2, e_r = 0, C = 1, α = 8, d* = 1, h = $β_1$, and γ = 20.5 dB.**

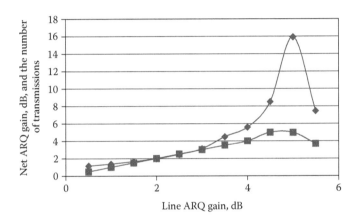

Figure 6.2 **Net ARQ gain (squares) and the number of transmissions (diamonds) versus the line ARQ gain at b = 15 bits, N = 300, R = 16, e_r = 0, C = 1, α = 8, d* = 1, h = $β_1$, and γ = 54 dB.**

Figure 6.1 presents the results of computing k and $μ_n$ for a set of $μ_1$ values obtained incrementally with a step of 0.5 dB. The channel is characterized by b = 3 bits, N = 60, R = 2, e_r = 0, C = 1, α = 8, $β_{d*}$ = h, d* = 1, k_1 = 1, and γ = 20.5 dB; the closure $ω(b) = 4/(3 + 2b)$ was used. The BER value for this channel is 4.6×10^{-21}. One can see that to find $μ_1$ corresponding to k = 2, one needs five steps. The net ARQ gain increases with increasing k up to 14; it starts decreasing at k > 14. Therefore, if the modem memory allows for it, the optimum k should be set to 14 and $μ_1$ ~ to 6.5 dB. Equation 6.3.11 shows that utilizing the ARQ gain at k_{opt} yields 75 percent increase in throughput.

Figure 6.2 presents the results of computing k and μ_n for a set of μ_l values obtained incrementally with a step of 0.5 dB. The channel is characterized by b = 15 bits, N = 300, R = 16, e_r = 0, C = 1, α = 8, β_{d*} = h, d* = 1, k_1 = 1, and γ = 54 dB. The BER value for this channel is 2.4 × 10^{-37}. The net ARQ gain increases with increasing k up to 8; it starts decreasing at k > 8. Here, the optimum k should be set to 8, and μ_l ~ to 5 dB. Utilizing the ARQ gain at k_{opt} yields 11 percent increase in throughput.

6.5 A Procedure for Determining the Optimum ARQ Parameters

Figure 6.3 presents the results of computing k and μ_n for a set of μ_l values obtained incrementally with a step of 0.5 dB. The channel is characterized by b = 3 bits, N = 60, R = 2, e_r = 0, C = 1, α = 8, β_{d*} = h, d* = 1, k_1 = 1, and γ = 16 dB. The BER value here is 3.6 × 10^{-7}. The net ARQ gain increases with increasing k up to 3; it starts decreasing at k > 3. Here, the optimum k should be set to 3, and the corresponding μ_l ~ to 2 dB. Utilizing the ARQ gain at k_{opt} yields 25 percent increase in throughput.

Note that here the channel parameters are the same as those in the calculation shown in Figure 6.1, except for the SNR. Comparing Figure 6.1 and Figure 6.3 shows that the difference in SNR values in both cases (4.5 dB) is approximately equal to the difference in the optimum (maximizing μ_n) values of μ_l.

Figure 6.4 presents the results of computing k and μ_n for a set of μ_l values obtained incrementally with a step of 0.5 dB. The channel is characterized by b = 15 bits, N = 300, R = 16, e_r = 0, C = 1, α = 8, β_{d*} = h, d* = 1, k_1 = 1, and γ = 49.8 dB. The BER value here is 0.8 × 10^{-7}. The net ARQ gain increases with increasing k up to 2 and it starts decreasing at k > 2. Here, the optimum k should be set to 2, and the corresponding μ_l ~ to 0.5 dB. Utilizing the ARQ gain at k_{opt} yields 2 percent increase in throughput.

Note that in this case the channel parameters are the same as those in the calculation shown in Figure 6.2, except for the SNR. Again, comparing Figure 6.2 and Figure 6.4 shows that the difference in SNR values in both cases (4.2 dB) is quite close to the difference in the optimum values of μ_l.

The surprising independence of the difference between the channel SNR and the optimum line ARQ gain on the channel SNR is not accidental; it will be formally proved in the following text.

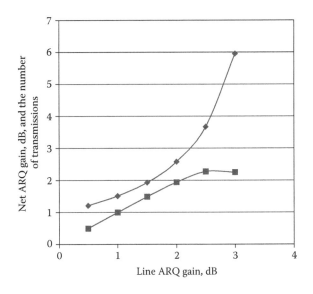

Figure 6.3 Net ARQ gain (squares) and the number of transmissions (diamonds) versus the line ARQ gain at b = 3 bits, N = 60, R = 2, e_r = 0, C = 1, α = 8, d* = 1, h = β_1, and γ = 16 dB.

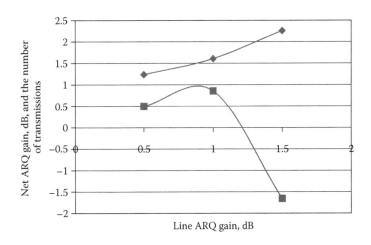

Figure 6.4 Net ARQ gain (squares) and the number of transmissions (diamonds) versus the line ARQ gain at b = 15 bits, N = 300, R = 16, e_r = 0, C = 1, α = 8, d* = 1, h = β_1, and γ = 49.8 dB.

Consider again two states of a QAM channel. In both states, the bit loads are identical at the same BER. In the first state, only FEC is applied to the channel, and the channel SNR is γ. In the second state, both FEC (with the same parameters) and k-ARQ are applied, and the channel SNR is $\gamma - \mu_1$. Let us look at the dependence of the net ARQ gain μ_n on the line ARQ gain μ_1, and let this dependence have a maximum at $\mu_{1,opt}$, and the corresponding value of k is k_{opt}. In the following text, we will prove that $\gamma - \mu_{1,opt}$ is invariant with respect to γ.

Using Equation 6.7.10, let us present Equation 6.3.10 in the following form:

$$10^{\mu_n/10} = \frac{10^{\gamma/10}}{1 - \frac{K + C + R}{t + 1}\alpha\varepsilon}\Omega\left(\gamma,\mu_1,k\left(\mu_1,\gamma\right)\right) \qquad (6.5.1)$$

where an auxiliary function $\Omega\left(\gamma,\mu_1,k\left(\mu_1,\gamma\right)\right)$ is defined as:

$$\Omega(\gamma,\mu_1,k(\mu_1,\gamma)) \equiv 10^{(\mu_1 - \gamma)/10}\left[1 - \left(\frac{K + C + R}{t + 1}\alpha\varepsilon\right)^{1/k(\mu_1,\gamma)}\right] \qquad (6.5.2)$$

Because ε in Equation 6.5.1 is the same for all $(\mu_1,k(\mu_1,\gamma))$ states, determining $\mu_{1,opt}$ for given γ is equivalent to maximizing the function $\Omega\left(\gamma,\mu_1,k\left(\mu_1,\gamma\right)\right)$ with respect to μ_1. We will show that although k is a function of both γ and μ_1, $\Omega\left(\gamma,\mu_1,k\left(\mu_1,\gamma\right)\right)$ in Equation 6.5.2 depends only on the difference $\gamma - \mu_1$ rather than on γ and μ_1 separately. Let us present Equation 6.2.8 in the following form:

$$\frac{K + C + R}{t + 1}\alpha\varepsilon = \left[\frac{\beta_{d^*}\alpha}{h}\left(\omega(b)p_{QAM}\right)^{d^*}\right]^{(t+1)k}$$

$$\left[\frac{\Gamma\left(K + C + R + 1\right)}{\Gamma\left(K + C + R - t\right)\Gamma(t + 2)}\right]^k \qquad (6.5.3)$$

Introducing Equation 6.3.2 in Equation 6.5.3 yields:

$$\frac{1}{k} \ln\left(\frac{K + C + R}{t + 1} \alpha\varepsilon\right) = \left(1 + \Theta\left(\gamma - \mu_1\right)\right)\ln$$

$$\left(\frac{\Gamma\left(K + C + R + 1\right)}{\Gamma\left(K + C + R - t\right)\Gamma(t + 2)}\right) \qquad (6.5.4)$$

Finally, using Equation 6.5.4, let us present Equation 6.5.2 as follows:

$$\Omega\left(\gamma - \mu_1\right) = 10^{(\mu_1-\gamma)/10}\left\{1 - \exp\left[\frac{\left(1 + \Theta\left(\gamma - \mu_1\right)\right)\ln}{\left(\frac{\Gamma\left(K + C + R + 1\right)}{\Gamma\left(K + C + R - t\right)\Gamma(t + 2)}\right)}\right]\right\} \qquad (6.5.5)$$

In Equation 6.5.5, Ω depends on $\gamma - \mu_1$ rather than on γ and μ_1. Because the value of argument maximizing the function $\Omega(...)$ does not depend on γ, $\gamma - \mu_{1,\text{opt}}$ is invariant with respect to μ. This completes the proof.

This result allows us to propose the following fast method of determining the optimum ARQ parameters at the actual channel conditions (i.e., for zero margin), based on their values at some reference conditions yielding a certain standard-stipulated BER (i.e., for actual margin).

Let the reference ARQ parameters correspond to a standard-stipulated BER. Let these reference conditions correspond to SNR equal to γ_1. The reference optimum ARQ parameters, $\mu_{1,\text{opt},1}$ and $k_{1,\text{opt}}$, should be either stored in the modem memory in a lookup table or calculated prior to channel initialization. The channel is characterized by the following actual parameters: γ_2, $\mu_{1,\text{opt},2}$, and $k_{2,\text{opt}}$, and by a different (smaller) BER. The margin value of $M = \gamma_2 - \gamma_1$ is used in the bit loading process, i.e., M is the difference between the actual and margin-adjusted SNR.

Given the $\mu_{1,\text{opt},1}$ value, $\mu_{1,\text{opt},2}$ can be found from the following equation:

$$\gamma_2 - \mu_{1,\text{opt},2} = \gamma_1 - \mu_{1,\text{opt},1} \qquad (6.5.6)$$

Equation 6.5.6 formalizes the result we just proved. The new optimum k is then obtained as follows:

$$k_{2,opt} = \frac{1 + \Theta(\gamma_2)}{1 + \Theta(\gamma_2 - \mu_{1,opt,2})} \tag{6.5.7}$$

Note that Equation 6.5.7 is nothing but Equation 6.3.8 written for actual channel conditions. Writing Equation 6.3.8 for reference conditions yields:

$$k_{1,opt} = \frac{1 + \Theta(\gamma_1)}{1 + \Theta(\gamma_1 - \mu_{1,opt,1})} \tag{6.5.8}$$

Finally, combining Equation 6.5.6 and Equation 6.5.8 yields the following relation between $k_{1,opt}$ and $k_{2,opt}$:

$$\frac{k_{2,opt}}{k_{1,opt}} = \frac{1 + \Theta(\gamma_2)}{1 + \Theta(\gamma_1)} \tag{6.5.9}$$

The dependence $\Theta(\gamma)$ should be stored in the modem memory as a lookup table.

If the reference optimum ARQ parameters are not stored in the modem memory, they need to be precalculated during the communication session prior to channel initialization. This has to be done at the standard-stipulated BER using the procedure described earlier. Then Equation 6.5.6 and Equation 6.5.7 (or Equation 6.5.6 and Equation 6.5.9) have to be applied for finding the actual optimum ARQ parameters. As the results presented in Figure 6.3 and Figure 6.4 show, the consequent search for the maximum of the net ARQ gain at $\varepsilon \sim 10^{-7}$ takes just a few incremental (0.5 dB) steps using Equation 6.3.1, compared to the cases shown in Figure 6.1 and Figure 6.2. This method is less expensive computationally, and it works faster than plainly incrementing μ_1, at zero margin, by $\Delta\mu_1$ until the μ_n maximum is reached.

At the end of this section, a useful relation between $\mu_{n,opt,1}$ and $\mu_{n,opt,2}$ will be derived. Combining Equation 6.5.1, Equation 6.5.5, and Equation 6.5.6 yields:

$$\left(\gamma_2 - \mu_{n,opt,2}\right) - \left(\gamma_1 - \mu_{n,opt,1}\right) = 10 \log \left[\frac{\left(1 - \frac{K + C + R}{t + 1} \frac{\alpha}{\beta} \varepsilon_2\right)}{\left(1 - \frac{K + C + R}{t + 1} \frac{\alpha}{\beta} \varepsilon_1\right)} \right] \tag{6.5.10}$$

At $N\varepsilon_1 \ll 1$ and $N\varepsilon_2 \ll 1$, the right-hand side of Equation 6.5.10 is $4.34 \cdot \left[N\alpha/(t+1)\beta \right]\left(\varepsilon_1 - \varepsilon_2\right) \ll 1$, and Equation 6.5.10 acquires the same form as Equation 6.5.6:

$$\gamma_2 - \mu_{n,opt,2} = \gamma_1 - \mu_{n,opt,1} \tag{6.5.11}$$

Comparing Figure 6.1 to Figure 6.4 does show that Equation 6.5.11 works well.

6.6 Extension of the Method for the Case of a Slowly Fading Channel

The model assumed in this chapter so far is an AWGN channel. Because a typical wireless channel suffers from fading in one way or another, it would be useful to account for fading in our derivations. For a slowly fading channel, Equation 6.2.7 becomes:

$$p_b = 0.1 \ln 10 \cdot \omega(b) \int_0^\infty \pi(\gamma,\gamma') \, p_{QAM}(\gamma') 10^{\gamma'/10} d\gamma' \tag{6.6.1}$$

where $\pi(\ldots,\ldots)$ is the probability density of γ when the attenuation factor of the channel is random (for Rayleigh fading channel , $\pi(\ldots,\ldots)$ is presented in [9], p.773). Equation 6.2.8 and Equation 6.3.2 become:

$$\varepsilon = \frac{1}{\alpha}\left[\left(0.1 \ln 10 \cdot \omega(b) \int_0^\infty \pi(\gamma,\gamma') \, p_{QAM}(\gamma') 10^{\gamma'/10} d\gamma' \right)^{d^*} \frac{\alpha\beta_{d^*}}{Wh} \right]^{(t+1)k} \tag{6.6.2}$$

$$\Theta(\gamma) = \cfrac{(t+1)\ln\dfrac{\alpha\beta_{d^*}}{h} + d^*(t+1)\ln\left[\cfrac{0.1 \ln 10 \cdot \omega(b)\displaystyle\int_0^\infty \pi(\gamma,\gamma')}{p_{QAM}(\gamma') 10^{\gamma'/10} d\gamma'} \right]}{\ln\left[\dfrac{\Gamma(K+C+R+1)}{\Gamma(K+C+R-t)\Gamma(t+2)} \right]} \tag{6.6.3}$$

The rest of the equations derived earlier remains the same.

6.7 Determining the Average Number of Transmissions and the Uncoded SER, Given the SER Past FEC/ARQ

First, let us consider a single RS code. At the SER level of ε_s,

$$\text{SER}\left(t,K,p_e\left(t,K\right)\right) = \varepsilon_S \ll 1 \qquad (6.7.1)$$

Using Equation 6.2.2 we can rewrite Equation 6.7.1 as:

$$\varepsilon_S = p_e^{(t+1)k}\left[\sum_{i=t+1}^{N} p_e^{i-t-1}\left(1-p_e\right)^{N-i}\binom{N-1}{i-1}\right]\left[\sum_{i=t+1}^{N} p_e^{i-t-1}\left(1-p_e\right)^{N-i}\binom{N}{i}\right]^{k-1} \qquad (6.7.2)$$

It can be reduced to the following form:

$$\varepsilon_S^{1/(t+1)k} = \frac{p_e}{w\left(p_e\right)} \qquad (6.7.3)$$

$$w(p_e)=\left[\sum_{i=t+1}^{N} p_e^{i-t-1}\left(1-p_e\right)^{N-i}\binom{N-1}{i-1}\right]^{\frac{-1}{(t+1)k}}\left[\sum_{i=t+1}^{N} p_e^{i-t-1}\left(1-p_e\right)^{N-i}\binom{N}{i}\right]^{\frac{-(k-1)}{(t+1)k}} \qquad (6.7.4)$$

Applying the Lagrange inversion theorem [12] to Equation 6.7.3 yields:

$$p_e = W\left(R,K,k\right)\varepsilon_S^{\frac{1}{(t+1)k}} + O\left(\varepsilon_S^{\frac{2}{(t+1)k}}\right), \ W\left(R,K,k\right) = w\left(0\right) \qquad (6.7.4)$$

From Equation 6.7.4 and using the equality $N = K + C + R$ it follows that

$$W(R,K,k) = \left[\binom{K+C+R-1}{t}\right]^{\frac{-1}{(t+1)k}}\left[\binom{K+C+R}{t+1}\right]^{\frac{-(k-1)}{(t+1)k}} \qquad (6.7.5)$$

Equation 6.2.6 is a continuous representation of Equation 6.7.5 in gamma functions.

Finally, the uncoded bit error rate p_b corresponding to p_e is found from the following formula:

$$p_e = 1 - (1 - p_b)^\alpha \qquad (6.7.6)$$

which, at $W(R,K,k)\varepsilon_S^{1/(t+1)k} \ll 1$ and using Equation 6.7.4, yields:

$$p_b = 1 - (1 - p_e)^{1/\alpha} = 1 - \left(1 - W(R,K,k)\varepsilon_S^{\frac{1}{(t+1)k}}\right)^{1/\alpha} \approx \frac{W(R,K,k)}{\alpha}\varepsilon_S^{\frac{1}{(t+1)k}} \qquad (6.7.7)$$

The average number of transmissions (Equation 6.2.3) could also be evaluated. One can write for p defined in Equation 6.2.1:

$$p = \sum_{i=0}^{t} p_e^i (1 - p_e)^{N-i} \binom{N}{i} = 1 - p_e^{t+1} \sum_{i=t+1}^{N} p_e^{i-t-1} (1 - p_e)^{N-i} \binom{N}{i} \qquad (6.7.8)$$

Combining Equation 6.7.8 with Equation 6.7.4 and Equation 6.7.5 yields:

$$p = 1 - W^{t+1}(R,K,k)\,\varepsilon_S^{\left(\frac{1}{k}\right)(K+C+R)}_{\quad t+1}\left[1 + O\left(\frac{1}{\varepsilon_S^{(t+1)k}}\right)\right] = 1 - \left[\frac{K+C+R}{t+1}\varepsilon_S\right]^{\frac{1}{k}} \qquad (6.7.9)$$

Introducing Equation 6.7.6 into Equation 6.2.3 yields

$$v = \frac{\left(1 - \dfrac{K+C+R}{t+1}\varepsilon_S\right)}{\left[1 - \left(\dfrac{K+C+R}{t+1}\varepsilon_S\right)^{\frac{1}{k}}\right]} \qquad (6.7.10)$$

The Lagrange inversion theorem allows one to obtain higher-order terms in Equation 6.7.4. For instance, in the case of $k = 1$ one has:

$$p_e = W(R,K)\varepsilon_S^{\frac{1}{t+1}} - \frac{K+C+R-t-1}{(t+1)^2}W^2(R,K)\varepsilon_S^{\frac{2}{t+1}}$$

$$+ O\left(\varepsilon_S^{\frac{3}{t+1}}\right), \ W(R,K) = w(0) \qquad (6.7.11)$$

But, as our calculations show, when applying the second-order correction (Equation 6.7.11) for typical parameters, this yields no more than 1 percent change in p_e.

For a concatenation of convolutional and RS codes, the Lagrange inversion theorem should be applied to an $\varepsilon_s(p_b)$ dependence defined by the following two equations:

$$\varepsilon_s = p_e^{(t+1)k}\left[\sum_{i=t+1}^{N} p_e^{i-t-1}\left(1-p_e\right)^{N-1}\binom{N-1}{i-1}\right]\left[\sum_{i=t+1}^{N} p_e^{i-t-1}\left(1-p_e\right)^{N-i}\binom{N}{i}\right]^{k-1} \quad (6.7.12)$$

$$1-\left(1-p_e\right)^{1/\alpha} = \frac{1}{h}\sum_{d=d^*}^{\infty}\beta_d p_b^d\sum_{m=0}^{d-1}\left(1-p_b\right)^m\binom{d-1+m}{m} \quad (6.7.13)$$

For small BER, the inversion yields:

$$p_b = \left(\frac{Wh}{\alpha\beta_{d^*}}\varepsilon_S^{\frac{1}{(t+1)k}}\right)^{1/d^*} \quad (6.7.14)$$

where W is defined by Equation 6.7.5. At $\beta_{d^*} = h$ and $d^* = 1$, Equation 6.7.14 transforms into Equation 6.7.7. Finally, as $p_e(\varepsilon_s)$ is still given by Equation 6.7.4, Equation 6.7.8 to Equation 6.7.10 remain the same.

6.8 Determining an Average Fraction of Erroneous Bits in an Erroneous QAM Symbol

Consider an arbitrary 2^b signal constellation on a square lattice. Let a_i be the binary representation of the label for the i-th point of the constellation. Let χ_i be the coordination number of this point, i.e., the total number of its nearest neighbor points. Then, the factor used to convert a QAM symbol error rate into a bit error rate, $\omega(b)$, can be calculated by the following formula:

$$\omega(b) = \frac{\left[\sum_{i=1}^{2^b}\sum_{j\neq i}^{\chi_i} d_H\left(a_i, a_j\right)/\chi_i\right]}{\left(b\cdot 2^b\right)} \quad (6.8.1)$$

Here, $d_H(\bullet, \bullet)$ is the Hamming distance between two binary vectors, and the innermost summation in Equation 6.8.1 is performed over the nearest neighbors of the point i.

The question about determining an average fraction of erroneous bits in an erroneous QAM symbol is considered in more detail in Chapter 8.

6.9 Conclusions

Methods presented in the preceding text evaluate k, μ_1, and μ_n on the same set of FEC parameters. This assumption may yield a suboptimal solution of the channel performance optimization problem.

Optimizing the channel performance with respect to both FEC and ARQ parameters comprises:

- For each allowable set of FEC parameters, compute (or extract from precalculated lookup tables) the corresponding net performance gain without ARQ.
- For each allowable set of FEC parameters, compute the corresponding net ARQ gain, given the maximum allowed number of transmissions.
- Compare all "net FEC gain + net ARQ gain" values, for all sets of FEC parameters, and find the maximum.

As the total number of allowable FEC parameter sets may be quite large (e.g., 10 to 20), there is always a small group (two or three) of closely competing (performance-wise) sets. One can determine from computations (or extract from precalculated tables), a few FEC parameter sets yielding the largest net performance gain without ARQ. Then, the methods described in the preceding text should be applied to these few sets.

It is straightforward to see that by replacing

$$\omega(b)p_{QAM}$$

in Equation 6.2.8 with an appropriate expression, the proposed method can be used for other types of modulation than QAM.

Summarizing the results in this chapter, for a QAM communication channel with FEC and ARQ, the BER is estimated as a function of the channel SNR. A method is presented for trading off the number of allowed transmissions and the level of margin (or the line ARQ gain) applied to the channel SNR. The line ARQ gain maximizing the channel throughput is shown to be a sum of the channel SNR and some function of the bit load and FEC parameters. Using this result, we formulate a fast method of determining the optimum ARQ parameters at the actual channel conditions, based on their values at some reference conditions, the latter being either stored in the modem memory or calculated prior to channel initialization. The derivations are presented both for AWGN and slowly fading channel conditions.

References

1. ETSI, Requirements and Architectures for Wireless Broadband Access, TR 101 031 V2.2.1, January 1999.
2. IEEE 802.16, Preliminary Draft Working Document for 802.16 Broadband Wireless Access System Requirements, IEEE 802.16s0-99/5, October 1999.
3. Chakraborty, S.S., Yli-Juuti, E., and Liinaharji, M., An ARQ scheme with packet combining, *IEEE Commun. Lett.*, Vol. 2(7), 200–202, July 1998.
4. Lambrette, U., Bruhl, L., and Meyr, H., ARQ protocol performance for a wireless high data rate link, *IEEE 47th VTC Proc.*, Vol. 3, pp. 1538–1542, May 1997.
5. Fukui, N., Shibuya, A., and Murakami, K., Performance of combined ARQ with SR and GBN for broadband wireless systems on a 40 GHz band radio channel, *IEEE Commun. Mag.*, Vol. 39(9), 122–126, September 2001.
6. Chen, W.Y., *DSL: Simulation Techniques and Standards Development for Digital Subscriber Line Systems*, Indianapolis: Macmillan Technical Publishing, 1998.
7. *ITU Recommendation G.992.2: Splitterless Asymmetric Digital Subscriber Line (ADSL) Transceivers*, Geneva, 1999.
8. Lee, L.H.C., *Convolutional Coding: Fundamentals and Applications*, Boston, MA: Artech House, 1997.
9. Proakis, J., *Digital Communications*, New York: McGraw-Hill, 1995.
10. MacWilliams, F.J., Sloane, N.J.A., *The Theory of Error-Correcting Codes*, Amsterdam: Elsevier Science, 1977.
11. Feher, K., *Wireless Digital Communications*, Upper Saddle River: Prentice-Hall, 1995.
12. de Bruijn, N.G., *Asymptotic Methods in Analysis*, New York: Dover Publications, 1981.
13. Mitlin, V., Williams, R.G.C., Performance Evaluation of Multicarrier Channels with Forward Error Correction and Automatic Repeat Request, U.S. Patent Application No. 20020108081, pending.

14. Mitlin, V., Williams, R.G.C., Performance Evaluation of Multicarrier Channels, U.S. Patent Application No. 20030105997, pending.
15. Mitlin, V., Mueller, J., Method and Apparatus for Selection of ARQ parameters and Estimation of Improved Communications, U.S. Patent No. 6,718,493, 2004.
16. Mitlin, V., Optimal selection of ARQ parameters in QAM channels, *J. Wirel. Commun. Mob. Comput.*, Vol. 5, 165–174; 2005.

Chapter 7

Optimal Selection of Error Correction and Retransmission Parameters in Multichannel Communications Systems

7.1 Background

In this chapter, we will discuss the method of performance optimization of multicarrier systems with forward error correction (FEC) and automatic repeat request (ARQ). The essence of the method is reducing the evaluation of the performance of a typical multicarrier channel to the evaluation of the performance of a single quadrature amplitude modulation (QAM) channel with the average parameters of all subchannels of that multicarrier channel. Although this technique has been applied before in very specific circumstances, it is generalized here to include many different FEC and ARQ scenarios and is found to be valid in all cases. The method is applied to a hypothetical Asymmetrical Digital Subscriber Line (ADSL) system, compliant with the ITU standards [1,2], to jointly optimize Reed–Solomon (RS) parameters and the maximum number of retransmissions allowed for a given channel and a desired error rate.

7.2 Performance Gain Due to FEC/ARQ in Discrete Multitone Systems

Consider a data transmission between two stations. The error-controlling algorithm uses a combination of an FEC code and a cyclic redundancy check (CRC). The forward error correction can be any type of code but here we will consider RS codes. Each information frame has a length of N code symbols containing an information field of length K symbols. The N − K redundant code symbols are divided into a CRC field of length C symbols and a parity check field of length R symbols, i.e., N = K + C + R. The number of correctable symbol errors, t, depends on R. The t-error correcting is assumed to correct all information frames that are received with no more than t errors. Also, for any frame with more than t errors, the CRC is assumed to always detect the residual errors after FEC. In this case, a negative acknowledgment frame will be sent to the peer, and the frame will be retransmitted. A limit of k is imposed on the number of frame transmissions (k = 1 indicates that no retransmissions will take place). A positive acknowledgment is sent to the peer for every m information frames correctly received. Our other simplifying assumptions are that no packets are lost in transmission and that all acknowledgment frames are received correctly.

In the following text, we will estimate the performance gain that particular FEC/ARQ parameters will achieve in such a communications system with a discrete multitone (DMT) modulation scheme.

DMT is a form of multicarrier modulation in which each carrier is assigned a number of bits depending on its own noise parameters. A DMT system can be thought of as n QAM modems. Each QAM waveform carries a binary array of b_i bits, i = 1, ..., n, in each symbol period and occupies one of the subchannels (bins) [3,4]. A DMT symbol is the superposition of these n waveforms carrying:

$$B_{DMT} = \sum_{i=1}^{n} b_i \qquad (7.2.1)$$

bits. Combining B_{DMT} with the system's DMT symbol rate gives the line data rate. Some of the bits transferred are used for the FEC and are not part of the net data rate that the user sees. A DMT system should be optimized for maximum net data rate under all conditions. In the ITU ADSL systems, this is reduced to a bit-loading problem because certain parameters are fixed. In these systems, the required bit error rate is 10^{-7} with a fixed margin. This means that the few RS coding options available in [1] can be analyzed to discover the coding gain given by each under these conditions. The coding scheme having the least redundancy yet maximizing the net data rate for the channel conditions measured will be selected, and a bit-loading technique assuming an uncoded error probability can be applied [5–7]. In general, when the error rate, margin, and decoding latency are all determined at the application layer, it is not possible for the DMT system designer to calculate all the necessary permutations in advance; an implementable method is needed to do this.

In Chapter 6, we derived a general equation (Equation 6.2.8) that involves the coding redundancy, average number of retransmissions, desired error rate, and bit loading of a QAM channel. For the case considered in this chapter, the unified equation for a single QAM subchannel with FEC/ARQ takes the form:

$$1 - \left(1 - W(t,K,k)\varepsilon_S^{\frac{1}{(t+1)k}}\right)^{\frac{1}{\alpha}} = \omega(b_i)\left(1 - 2^{-b_i/2}\right)\mathrm{erfc}\left(\sqrt{\frac{3 \cdot 10^{\gamma_i/10}}{2^{b_i+1} - 2}}\right)$$
$$\times \left[2 - \left(1 - 2^{-b_i/2}\right)\mathrm{erfc}\left(\sqrt{\frac{3 \cdot 10^{\gamma_i/10}}{2^{b_i+1} - 2}}\right)\right] \qquad (7.2.2)$$

Here b_i is the number of bits per bin, $1/\omega(b) = (2b+3)/4$ is the factor used to convert an individual QAM symbol error rate into a bit error rate (see Chapter 8 for more details), γ_i is the signal-to-noise ratio (SNR) in dB of the i-th bin, and ε_s is the symbol error rate (SER) of the RS code in the system:

$$\varepsilon_S = 1 - (1 - \varepsilon/\beta)^{\alpha} \approx \alpha\varepsilon/\beta, \text{ as } \varepsilon \ll 1 \qquad (7.2.3)$$

where α is the number of bits per RS symbol, β is approximately equal to the number of nonzero coefficients in the scrambler polynomial, ε is the bit error rate required for the data, and

$$W(t,K,k) = \left[\binom{N-1}{t}\right]^{-\frac{1}{(t+1)k}}\left[\binom{N}{t+1}\right]^{-\frac{k-1}{(t+1)k}} \qquad (7.2.4)$$

Equation 7.2.2 has to be solved numerically. From this equation, the parameters that affect the performance of a system can be calculated. Specifically, given a desired bit error rate, ε, and a bit loading that fits the channel, the FEC and ARQ parameters that maximize the net coding gain of the system can be chosen (the extra information throughput per DMT symbol achieved through the use of FEC/ARQ):

$$G_n\left(t,K,k\right) \equiv \frac{K}{K + C + R}\frac{B_{DMT}\left(t,K,k\right)}{v} - \frac{K}{K + C}B_{DMT}\left(0,K,1\right) \quad (7.2.5)$$

where $B_{DMT}(t,K,k)$ is the bit size of a DMT symbol in a system with a t-symbol FEC, K information symbols, and a maximum of k transmissions per frame. The factor $K/(K + C + R)$ in Equation 7.2.5 takes the FEC redundancy into account. An important feature of Equation 7.2.5 is the presence of the average number of transmissions for a frame, v, defined earlier in Equation 6.2.3 and Equation 6.7.10. The factor v accounts for ARQ performance gain.

The ITU ADSL standards call for the chosen line data rate transferred during training so that both modems will be able to receive the data correctly. Therefore we need to know the total increase in the number of bits sent with one DMT symbol due to FEC/ARQ, or the line coding gain, which is:

$$G_l\left(t,K,k\right) \equiv B_{DMT}\left(t,K,k\right) - B_{DMT}\left(0,K,1\right) \quad (7.2.6)$$

For implementation efficiency, as Equation 7.2.2 applies to each individual QAM channel, it is desirable to find an equation applicable to the system as a whole. This equation is derived in Section 7.3.

7.3 Mean-Field Approximation for Multicarrier Channel with ARQ

It has been shown before [6–9] that it is possible to justify averaging the SNR across all bins and using this as an effective parameter in bit-loading algorithms for the uncoded case without ARQ. This works well for the current ADSL standards. If one wants to generalize the use of DMT systems to include ARQ schemes and to permit arbitrary error parameters chosen by the application using the modulation scheme, it is not obvious that this approximation still holds. As we show in the following text, it does. Specifically, the following mean-field approximation can be introduced:

$$B_{DMT} = \sum_{i=1}^{n_{eff}} b(\gamma_i) \approx n_{eff} b(\gamma_{eff})$$ (7.3.1)

which drastically reduces the complexity of the performance evaluation of a DMT channel. In Equation 7.3.1:

$$n_{eff} = \sum_{\gamma_i > \gamma_*} 1, \quad \gamma_{eff} = \frac{\sum_{\gamma_i > \gamma_*} \gamma_i}{n_{eff}}$$ (7.3.2)

and γ_* is the threshold level of SNR in dB below which no information can be passed.

Approximations (Equation 7.3.1 to Equation 7.3.2) allow one to evaluate the channel performance as follows. First, measurements of the channel SNR are made at different carrier frequencies. Next, the total number of usable carriers, n_{eff}, and an effective SNR for the channel, γ_{eff}, are determined using Equation 7.3.2. For these n_{eff} and γ_{eff}, Equation 7.2.2 is solved at different t and K and the solution, combined with Equation 7.3.1, yields the maximum number of information bits supported by a DMT symbol within the system's constraints. The corresponding net and line coding gain values per bin are:

$$g_n(t,K,k) \equiv \frac{G_n(t,K,k)}{n_{eff}}$$

$$= \frac{K}{K+C+R} \frac{b(\gamma_{eff},t,K,k)}{v} - \frac{K}{K+C} b(\gamma_{eff},0,K,1)$$ (7.3.3)

$$g_l(t,K,k) \equiv \frac{G_l(t,K,k)}{n_{eff}} = b(\gamma_{eff},t,K,k) - b(\gamma_{eff},0,K,1)$$ (7.3.4)

It was shown in [6–9] that the mean-field approximation is valid for multicarrier channels without FEC and ARQ. However, its validity is not obvious in the presence of FEC and ARQ. To show its validity, the following approximate solution of Equation 7.2.2 is derived in the next section:

$$b = \frac{\left[\gamma + \Phi(\gamma)\right]}{10\log 2}, \qquad (7.3.5)$$

$$\Phi(\gamma) = 10 \log \left\{ 10^{-\frac{\gamma}{10}} + \frac{3 \log e}{\left[2\log\left[\frac{\alpha\langle\omega(b)\rangle\sqrt{\frac{2}{\pi}}}{W(t,K,k)\left(\frac{\alpha\varepsilon}{\beta}\right)^{\frac{1}{(t+1)k}}} \right] - \log\log\left[\frac{\alpha\langle\omega(b)\rangle\sqrt{\frac{8}{\pi e^2}}}{W(t,K,k)\left(\frac{\alpha\varepsilon}{\beta}\right)^{\frac{1}{(t+1)k}}} \right] \right]} \right\} \qquad (7.3.6)$$

The accuracy of Equation 7.3.5 was tested by comparing the values of b given by Equation 7.3.5 to the ones found from numerically solving Equation 7.2.2. In our calculations, K varied between 16 and 256, γ varied between 10 and 50 dB, t varied between 0 and 8, b_{max} was equal to 15, and k was equal to 1 or 2. Results for K = 16 and 256 are presented in Figure 7.1 and Figure 7.2. The highest approximation error (a relative error between estimates of b obtained from Equation 7.3.5 and Equation 7.2.2) of around 5 percent is attained at the lowest K, lowest γ, and highest t. For the same t, larger γ values yield lower errors and the error also decreases as K increases. Equation 7.3.5 and Equation 7.3.6 work well in the SNR range considered.

It was found that for b ≥ 3, a simpler approximate solution of Equation 7.2.2 can be used:

$$b = \frac{\gamma + \phi}{10\log 2}, \quad \phi = \Phi(\infty) \qquad (7.3.7)$$

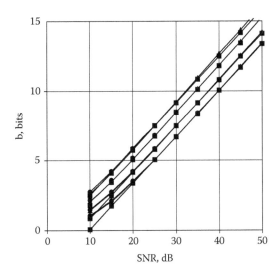

Figure 7.1 Results of computing the number of bits per bin by SNR at $\varepsilon =$ 10^{-7}, $\beta = 3$, $\alpha = 8$, C = 0, and K = 16; four groups, each consisting of three curves, are shown; specifically, from bottom to the top: k = 1, t = 0; k = 2, t = 0; k = 2, t = 2; and k = 2, t = 8; triangles, circles, and squares correspond to Equation 7.2.2, Equation 7.3.5, and Equation 7.3.7, respectively.

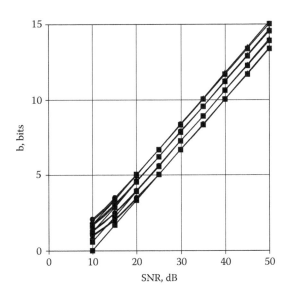

Figure 7.2 Same as Figure 7.1 but K = 256.

Results obtained from this approximation for K = 16 and 256 are also presented in Figure 7.1 and Figure 7.2 (shown by straight lines). Here, the highest relative error was attained at the lowest K and the lowest t, and it was always less than 5 percent (for b ≥ 3). As before, for the same t, larger γ values yielded smaller errors, and the error also decreases as K increases. For values of b ~ 3, Equation 7.3.7 gives b with an error of about 0.1 and this error decreases as γ increases. This means that, for a not very poor quality channel (in which most of the bins carry at least 3 bits), the mean-field approximation is valid as the relationship between b and γ is linear in Equation 7.3.7, and all the effects of FEC and ARQ are incorporated in the free term of that linear relationship:

$$
B_{DMT} = \sum_{i=1}^{n_{eff}} b(\gamma_i) \approx \left(\frac{\sum_{i=1}^{n_{eff}} (\gamma_i + \phi)}{10 \log 2} \right)
$$

$$
= n_{eff} \left[\left(\phi + \frac{\left(\dfrac{\sum_{i=1}^{n_{eff}} \gamma_i}{n_{eff}} \right)}{10 \log 2} \right) \right] = n_{eff} b(\gamma_{eff})
\tag{7.3.8}
$$

Moreover, the solution of Equation 7.3.7 allows one to apply the same line coding gain, g_l, to all bins.

7.4 An Approximate Solution of Equation 7.2.2

Let us present Equation 7.2.2 at small ε_s in the following form:

$$
\text{erfc}\left(\sqrt{\frac{1.5 \cdot 10^{\gamma/10}}{2^b - 1}} \right) = \frac{1 - \left[1 - W(t, K, k) \varepsilon_s^{\frac{1}{(t+1)k}} \right]^{1/\alpha}}{2\omega(b)(1 - 2^{-b/2})}
\tag{7.4.1}
$$

Also, at small ε_s one can apply the following asymptotic relation:

$$\text{erfc}(x) = \left(\frac{\exp(-x^2)}{x \pi^{\frac{1}{2}}} \right) \left[1 + O\left(x^{-2} \right) \right], \quad \text{as} \quad x \to \infty$$

which yields:

$$x \exp x = \frac{8\omega^2(b)\left(1 - 2^{-b/2} \right)^2}{\pi} \left[1 - \left(1 - W\left(t, K, k\right) \varepsilon_S^{\frac{1}{(t+1)k}} \right)^{1/\alpha} \right]^2,$$

$$x = \frac{3 \cdot 10^{\gamma/10}}{2^b - 1}$$

(7.4.2)

Equation 7.4.2 has the following asymptotic solution [10]:

$$x = \ln \left(\frac{8\omega^2(b)\left(1 - 2^{-b/2}\right)^2}{\pi \left[1 - \left(1 - W\left(t,K,k\right)\varepsilon_S^{\frac{1}{(t+1)k}} \right)^{1/\alpha} \right]^2} \right)$$

$$- \ln \ln \left(\frac{8\omega^2(b)\left(1 - 2^{-b/2}\right)^2}{\pi \left[1 - \left(1 - W\left(t,K,k\right)\varepsilon_S^{\frac{1}{(t+1)k}} \right)^{1/\alpha} \right]^2} \right)$$

(7.4.3)

At small ε_s and at $1 < b < b_{max}$ (b_{max} is the maximum bit load per bin allowed), replacing the $\omega(b)\left(1 - 2^{-b/2}\right)$ term in Equation 7.4.3 by

$$\langle \omega(b) \rangle = \left(\frac{\int_1^{b_{max}} \omega(b)\left(1 - 2^{-b/2}\right) db}{b_{max}} \right)$$

yields:

$$\frac{3 \cdot 10^{\gamma/10}}{2^b - 1} = 2\ln\left\{\frac{\langle\omega(b)\rangle\sqrt{\frac{8}{\pi}}}{1 - \left(1 - W(t, K, k)\varepsilon_S^{\frac{1}{(t+1)k}}\right)^{1/\alpha}}\right\}$$

$$- \ln\ln\left\{\frac{\langle\omega(b)\rangle\sqrt{\frac{8}{\pi}}}{1 - \left(1 - W(t, K, k)\varepsilon_S^{\frac{1}{(t+1)k}}\right)^{1/\alpha}}\right\} - \ln 2 \qquad (7.4.4)$$

Applying Equation 7.2.3 to Equation 7.4.4 yields a solution of Equation 7.2.2 in the form of Equation 7.3.5 and Equation 7.3.6.

7.5 Optimization of FEC and ARQ Parameters for Current ADSL Standards

The ITU ADSL standards [1,2] do not support ARQ. The effect of using ARQ to optimize the throughput of a G.992.2-compliant ADSL modem is considered in the following.

In G.992.2, the following restrictions on B_{DMT}, N, and R exist:

$$\frac{sB_{DMT}}{\alpha} = K + C + R, \quad R = zs, \quad C = s \qquad (7.5.1)$$

where s is the number of DMT symbols in an FEC frame and z is the number of FEC control symbols in a DMT symbol. There are 13 pairs of (z, s) in G.992.2. Introducing Equation 7.2.1 into Equation 7.5.1 yields:

$$b(\gamma_{eff}) = \frac{\alpha(K + s + zs)}{sn_{eff}} \qquad (7.5.2)$$

Combining Equation 7.5.2 and Equation 7.2.2 to Equation 7.2.4 yields:

$$\left[\frac{\alpha\left(K + s + zs\right)}{sn_{eff}} + 1.5\right]\left[1 - \left(1 - W\left(t, K, k\right)\varepsilon_S^{1/(1+zs/2)k}\right)^{1/\alpha}\right]$$

$$= 2\cdot erfc\left(\sqrt{\left(2^{\frac{1.5\cdot 10^{\gamma_{eff}/10}}{\frac{\alpha\left(K + s + zs\right)}{sn_{eff}}}} - 1\right)}\right)$$

$$\times\left[2 - \left(1 - 2^{-\frac{\alpha\left(K + s + zs\right)}{2sn_{eff}}}\right)erfc\left(\sqrt{\left(2^{\frac{1.5\cdot 10^{\gamma_{eff}/10}}{\frac{\alpha\left(K + s + zs\right)}{sn_{eff}}}} - 1\right)}\right)\right]$$

$$\times\left(1 - 2^{-\frac{\alpha\left(K+s+zs\right)}{2sn_{eff}}}\right)$$

(7.5.3)

where t is the number of correctable errors.

Equation 7.5.3 was solved numerically for K at different (z,s) pairs, γ_{eff}, n_{eff}, and k. K was treated as a continuous variable, and the factorials in W(...) were presented as logarithms of the gamma function. For each γ_{eff} and n_{eff}, the values of the net coding gain, g_n, were further determined from Equation 7.5.3 and Equation 7.3.3 and compared for all possible integer (k, z, s) triplets. The triplet providing the maximal g_n was found, and the corresponding line coding gain, g_l, was calculated.

Table 7.1 shows the best (s,z,g_l,k) set calculated at different n_{eff} and γ_{eff} values. As in the case without ARQ, shown for comparison in Table 7.2, the $g_l(n_{eff}, \gamma_{eff})$ dependence has discontinuities where one of the integer values (s,z,k) changes. This behavior follows from the procedure of determining g_l. By definition, as the optimal g_n is a continuous function of (n_{eff}, γ_{eff}), g_l has jumps exactly where the best g_n value is attained by two different (s, z) pairs.

One can see that the optimum ARQ strategy typically requires only one retransmission, k = 2. At low SNR (~10 dB), two or more retransmissions may be needed.

7.6 Conclusions

In this chapter, we considered a general multicarrier system with FEC and ARQ parameters. The problem of optimal selection of these parameters was explicitly solved. This problem has been solved before,

Table 7.1   Optimum FEC/ARQ Parameters (s/z/g$_i$/k) Calculated for a Hypothetical G.992.2 Modem at Different n$_{eff}$ and γ$_{eff}$ Values

n$_{eff}$ \ γ$_{eff}$	10	20	30	40	50
1	1/0/0.0/1	1/0/0.0/1	1/0/2.7/7	1/0/2.3/5	1/0/2.0/4
6	1/0/1.7/8	1/0/1.7/5	1/0/1.6/4	1/0/1.3/3	1/0/1.3/3
11	1/0/1.4/7	1/0/1.4/4	1/0/1.5/4	1/0/1.2/3	1/0/1.2/3
16	1/0/1.2/6	1/0/1.4/4	8/1/1.6/2	8/1/1.6/2	8/1/1.5/2
21	1/0/1.2/6	16/1/1.6/2	8/1/1.5/2	8/1/1.5/2	4/1/1.4/2
26	1/0/1.1/6	8/1/1.6/3	8/1/1.5/2	4/1/1.3/2	4/1/1.3/2
31	16/1/1.2/3	8/1/1.5/3	8/1/1.4/2	4/2/1.6/2	4/2/1.5/2
36	16/1/1.2/3	8/2/1.6/2	4/2/1.6/2	4/2/1.5/2	2/2/1.4/2
41	16/1/1.1/3	8/2/1.6/2	4/2/1.5/2	4/2/1.5/2	2/2/1.4/2
46	16/1/1.1/3	8/2/1.6/2	4/2/1.5/2	2/2/1.4/2	2/2/1.3/2
51	8/2/1.2/3	4/2/1.6/3	4/2/1.5/2	2/2/1.3/2	2/2/1.3/2
56	8/2/1.2/3	4/2/1.5/3	4/2/1.5/2	2/2/1.3/2	2/2/1.3/2
61	8/2/1.2/3	4/2/1.5/3	4/2/1.4/2	2/4/1.6/2	2/4/1.5/2
66	8/2/1.2/3	4/4/1.7/2	2/4/1.6/2	2/4/1.5/2	2/4/1.5/2
71	8/2/1.2/3	4/4/1.6/2	2/4/1.6/2	2/4/1.5/2	1/4/1.4/2
76	8/2/1.2/3	4/4/1.6/2	2/4/1.5/2	2/4/1.5/2	1/4/1.4/2
81	8/2/1.1/3	4/4/1.6/2	2/4/1.5/2	2/4/1.5/2	1/4/1.4/2
86	8/2/1.1/3	4/4/1.6/2	2/4/1.5/2	2/4/1.5/2	1/4/1.3/2
91	8/2/1.1/3	4/4/1.6/2	2/4/1.5/2	1/4/1.4/2	1/4/1.3/2
96	8/2/1.1/3	4/4/1.6/2	2/4/1.5/2	1/4/1.3/2	1/4/1.3/2

Note: Number of effective bins runs from 1 to 96; an effective SNR runs from 10 to 50 dB; e$_r$ = 0; number of transmissions varied between 1 and 10.

within the constraints of current multicarrier standards, by many implementers, and solutions have been documented by many authors [5–9]. Here, we consider the case in which FEC and ARQ parameters may be chosen from a large range of possibilities and the desired operating environment of the modem is not known *a priori*.

Table 7.2   Optimum FEC Parameters (s/z/g$_i$) Calculated for G.992.2 Modem at Different n$_{eff}$ and γ$_{eff}$ Values

n$_{eff}$ \ γ$_{eff}$	10	20	30	40	50
1	1/0/0.0	1/0/0.0	1/0/0.0	1/0/0.0	1/0/0.0
6	1/0/0.0	16/1/1.7	16/1/1.7	16/1/1.7	16/1/1.7
11	16/1/1.2	16/1/1.6	16/1/1.6	16/1/1.6	8/1/1.3
16	16/1/1.1	16/1/1.5	8/1/1.3	8/1/1.3	8/1/1.2
21	16/1/1.1	16/1/1.4	8/1/1.2	8/1/1.2	4/1/1.0
26	16/1/1.0	16/1/1.4	8/2/1.5	4/2/1.3	4/2/1.3
31	16/1/1.0	8/2/1.5	8/2/1.5	4/2/1.3	4/2/1.3
36	16/1/1.0	8/2/1.5	4/2/1.3	4/2/1.2	2/2/1.0
41	16/1/1.0	8/2/1.4	4/2/1.2	4/2/1.2	2/2/1.0
46	16/1/0.9	8/2/1.4	4/4/1.6	4/1/0.9	2/4/1.3
51	16/1/0.9	8/2/1.4	4/4/1.5	2/4/1.3	2/4/1.3
56	16/1/0.9	4/4/1.5	4/4/1.5	2/4/1.3	2/4/1.3
61	16/1/0.9	4/4/1.5	4/4/1.5	2/4/1.3	2/4/1.3
66	16/1/0.9	4/4/1.5	2/4/1.3	2/4/1.3	2/4/1.2
71	8/2/1.0	4/4/1.5	2/4/1.3	2/4/1.2	2/2/0.9
76	8/2/1.0	4/4/1.4	2/4/1.3	2/4/1.2	1/4/1.0
81	8/2/1.0	4/4/1.4	2/4/1.2	2/4/1.2	1/4/1.0
86	8/2/1.0	4/4/1.4	2/4/1.2	2/4/1.2	1/4/0.9
91	8/2/0.9	4/4/1.4	2/4/1.2	2/4/1.2	1/8/1.3
96	8/2/0.9	4/4/1.4	2/8/1.6	1/8/1.3	1/8/1.3

Note: Number of effective bins runs from 1 to 96; effective SNR runs from 10 to 50 dB; e$_r$ = 0.

The results obtained by practical approximations to this theory have been presented and their validity has been found to be within an acceptable range. The results have been applied to the hypothetical inclusion of ARQ in the current ADSL standards; it was shown that, in most cases, allowing a single retransmission will yield the optimum performance of these systems.

References

1. *ITU Recommendation G.992.2: Splitterless Asymmetric Digital Subscriber Line (ADSL) Transceivers*, Geneva, 1999.
2. Lin, S., Costello, D.J., Jr., and Miller, M.J., Automatic repeat request error control schemes, *IEEE Commun. Mag.*, Vol. 22(12), pp. 5–17, December 1984,.
3. Bingham, J.A.C., Multicarrier modulation for data transmission: an idea whose time has come, *IEEE Commun. Mag.*, Vol. 28, pp. 5–14, May 1990.
4. Chen, W.Y., *DSL: Simulation Techniques and Standards Development for Digital Subscriber Line Systems*, Indianapolis: Macmillan Technical Publishing, 1998.
5. Chow, P.S., Cioffi, J.M., and Bingham, J.A.C., A practical discrete multitone transceiver loading algorithm for data transmission over spectrally shaped channels, *IEEE Trans. Commun.*, Vol. 43, pp. 773–775, February/March/April 1995.
6. I. Kalet, The multitone channel, *IEEE Trans. Commun.*, Vol. COM-37, 119–124, 1989.
7. Chow, P.S., Bandwidth Optimized Digital Transmission Techniques for Spectrally Shaped Channels with Impulse Noise, Ph.D. thesis, Stanford University, May 1993.
8. Zervos, N.A., Kalet, I., Optimized decision feedback equilization versus optimized orthodonal frequency division multiplexing for high-speed data transmission over the local cable network, *Proc. ICC'89*, Boston, pp. 1080–1085, September 1989.
9. Fisher, R.F.H., Huber, J.B., On the equivalence of single- and multicarrier modulation: a new view, IEEE *Int. Symp. on Information Theory (ISIT '97)*, p. 197, Ulm, June–July 1997.
10. de Bruijn, N.G., *Asymptotic Methods in Analysis*, New York: Dover Publications, 1981.
11. Proakis, J.G., *Digital Communications*, New York: McGraw-Hill, 1995.
12. Mitlin, V., Williams, R.G.C., Performance Evaluation of Multicarrier Channels with Forward Error Correction and Automatic Repeat Request, U.S. Patent Application No. 20020108081, pending.
13. Mitlin, V., Williams, R.G.C., Performance Evaluation of Multicarrier Channels, U.S. Patent Application No. 20030105997, pending.
14. Mitlin, V., Mueller, J., Method and Apparatus for Selection of ARQ parameters and Estimation of Improved Communications, U.S. Patent No. 6,718,493, 2004.
15. Mitlin, V., Optimal selection of ARQ parameters in QAM channels, *J. Wirel. Commun. Mob. Comput.*, Vol. 5, 165–174; 2005.

Chapter 8

Bit Error Rate of Self-Similar Constellations in ADSL Systems

8.1 Background

In this chapter, the procedure of estimating the bit error rate in Asymmetrical Digital Subscriber Line (ADSL) systems is further discussed. Probabilistic properties of *quadrature amplitude modulation* (QAM) constellation encoders are determined using geometrical self-similarity of ADSL constellations with respect to the Hamming distance distribution. For large constellation sizes, probabilistic properties of odd-bit (nonsquare) constellation encoders can be described with the same equations that are used for even-bit (square) constellation encoders.

8.2 Self-Similarity of ADSL QAM Constellations

Current ADSL standards require, in the absence of the forward error correction block in the transceiver, the largest bit error rate (BER) value allowed past the demodulation stage p_b of 10^{-7}. For each ADSL QAM subchannel, the BER $\varepsilon = \omega \cdot p_{QAM}$ should not exceed p_b. Here, ω is an average fraction of erroneous bits in an erroneous QAM symbol; and

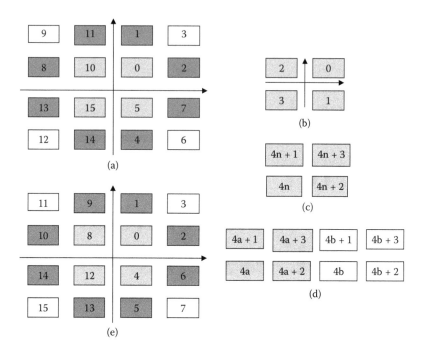

Figure 8.1 (a) ADSL ITU G.992.2 QAM constellation labeling for b = 4 [2]; the cardinality is 4 for each internal, 3 for each external noncorner, and 2 for each external corner points; (b) ADSL QAM constellation labeling at b = 2 is shown; (c) expansion of point n into the next larger square constellation; (d) construction used in Proposition 8.2; (e) Gray code constellation labeling for b = 4.

P_{QAM} is the QAM symbol error rate. Although an expression for P_{QAM} is known from communication theory ([1], p. 280) an expression for ω can be derived by considering nearest neighbors of a given correct constellation point as the only possible points obtained in error. Specifically, consider an arbitrary 2^b-point constellation on a square lattice (Figure 8.1a). Let a_i be the binary representation of the label for the i-th constellation point. Define χ_i as a set of label indices of the neighbors of the i-th point and $|\chi_i|$ as the cardinality of this point. For even-bit ADSL QAM constellations [2], the constellation-encoding procedure consists in selecting an odd integer point from the square-grid constellation based on the binary b-bit array, or tuple, $\{v_{b-1}, v_{b-2}, \ldots, v_1, v_0\}$. These b bits are identified with an integer label whose binary representation is $\{v_{b-1}, v_{b-2}, \ldots, v_1, v_0\}$. For example, for b = 2, the four constellation points are labeled 0, 1, 2, 3 (Figure 8.1b). The x- and y-coordinates of the constellation point are determined from the b bits $\{v_{b-1}, v_{b-2}, \ldots, v_1, v_0\}$, having 2's complement binary representations $\{v_{b-1}, v_{b-3}, \ldots, v_1, 1\}$ and $\{v_{b-2}, v_{b-4}, \ldots, v_0, 1\}$, respectively. The most significant bits are the sign bits for x- and y-coordinates.

ADSL QAM (b + 2)-bit constellations (Figure 8.1a) can be constructed recursively from b-bit constellations by replacing each label n by a 2 × 2 block of labels (Figure 8.1c). This forms the basis for studying their probabilistic properties. It is natural to assume that a decoding error yields any of the nearest neighbors of the constellation point i with equal probability of $1/|\chi_i|$.

Proposition 8.1

If a, b, c, d, and n are integers such that $c < 2^n$, $d < 2^n$, and $d_H(\ldots, \ldots)$ is the Hamming distance between the binary representations of two integers, then

$$d_H(2^n a + c, 2^n b + d) = d_H(a,b) + d_H(c,d)$$

The next proposition follows from Proposition 8.1.

Proposition 8.2

Let a and b be the labels of two neighbor points with the Hamming distance of $d_H(a,b)$ in a 2n-bit QAM constellation. Let a (2n + 2)-bit constellation be generated from a 2n-bit constellation according to the rule shown in Figure 8.1d. Then the Hamming distance between two neighbor points of two different 2 × 2 blocks generated from a and b is equal to $d_H(a,b) + 1$.

Proposition 8.1 and Proposition 8.2 allow one to describe properties of ADSL QAM constellations geometrically. Figure 8.2a shows a quarter of an eight-bit constellation. Little squares represent the constellation points. Crosses marked with a natural number n represent the boundaries separating any two points with the Hamming distance of n. For instance, if a decoding error yields a point lying across the four-error-boundary, the incorrect decoding yields four bit errors. The constellation shown in Figure 8.2a has one four-error-cross of the linear size 16, four three-error-crosses of the linear size 8, 4^2 two-error-crosses of the linear size 4, and so on. There is a central cross in each square block, and the constellation neighbors separated by that cross have the maximal d_H in that block. Each of the four subblocks of a square block with the n-error central cross repeats the pattern having an (n − 1)-error central cross.

Another way to think about the properties of ADSL QAM constellation encoders is by looking at the d_H distribution along a horizontal

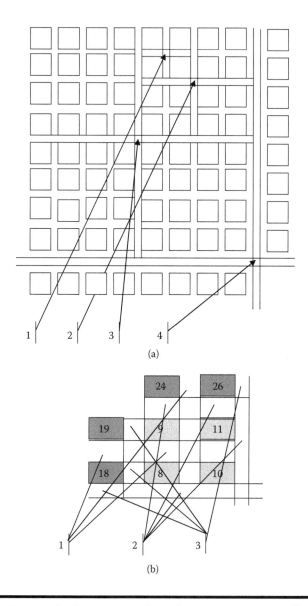

Figure 8.2 Geometrical representation of ADSL QAM constellation encoders; Hamming distances of 1, 2, and 3 between the adjacent constellation points are shown by arrows; (a) quarter of 256-point constellation; (b) quarter of 32-point constellation.

(or vertical) line in a constellation. In the 2^4-point constellation, it is {1, 2, 1}. In a larger 2^{b+2}-point square constellation, it can be generated from the distribution in a smaller 2^b-point constellation by increasing the values in the latter distribution by one and then inserting 1's in the beginning, between each two neighbors, and in the end.

Figure 8.2a shows that the d_H distribution repeats itself on smaller scales, i.e., it is self-similar, which will be used for determining probabilistic properties of ADSL QAM constellations.

8.3 Error Probability Function of an ADSL QAM Constellation Encoder

For a square b-bit ADSL QAM constellation (b = 2N), the probability of having k bit errors in an erroneously decoded tuple is determined as follows:

$$p(k,b) = \frac{1}{2^b} \sum_{i=1}^{2^b} \frac{1}{|\chi_i|} \sum_{j \in \chi_i} \delta_{d_H(a_i,a_j),k} \qquad (8.3.1)$$

where δ_{ij} is the Kronecker symbol. Let us call an edge starting at the constellation point i and ending in a nearest neighbor point j the (i,j)-link, and define the weight of the (i,j)-link as $1/|\chi_i|$. Under the nearest-neighbor-error supposition, the maximum number of errors that can be made in an erroneously decoded tuple is N. One can see that p(N,b) is contributed by all the links intersecting the central cross of the $2^N \times 2^N$ square. This yields:

$$p(N,b) = \frac{1}{2^{2N}} \left[\frac{1}{4} \cdot 4 \cdot 2^N + 8 \left(\frac{1}{3} - \frac{1}{4} \right) \right] \qquad (8.3.2)$$

Equation 8.3.2 accounts for the fact that eight links, corresponding to four endpoints of the cross, have the weight of 1/3, not 1/4. Generally, at k = N − i > 1, p(N − i,b) is contributed by all the links intersecting central crosses of the 4^i adjacent squares with the sizes $2^{N-i} \times 2^{N-i}$ forming our b-bit constellation:

$$p(N - i,b) = \frac{1}{2^{2N}} \left[2^{N+i} + 8 \left(\frac{1}{3} - \frac{1}{4} \right) 2^i \right], 0 \leq i \leq N - 2 \quad (8.3.3)$$

At k = 1, the probability is determined as follows:

$$p(1,b) = 1 - \sum_{i=0}^{N-2} p(N-i,b) = \frac{1}{2^{2N}}\left[2^{2N-1} + \frac{4}{3}\cdot 2^{N-1} + \frac{2}{3}\right] \quad (8.3.4)$$

Finally, noting that in the preceding equations, $i = b/2 - k$ and $N = b/2$ yields:

$$p(k,b) = \frac{1}{2^k}\left[1 + \frac{2}{3\cdot 2^{\frac{b}{2}}}\right] + \frac{1}{2^k}\frac{2}{3}\left[\frac{1}{2^{\frac{b}{2}}} + \frac{2}{2^b}\right]\delta_{1k}$$

$$= \frac{1}{2^k}\left[1 + O\!\left(\frac{1}{2^{\frac{b}{2}}}\right)\right], \quad 1 \le k \le \frac{b}{2}$$
(8.3.5)

The quantity $\omega(b)$ and the variance of the number of bit errors n_e in an erroneous tuple are:

$$\omega(b) = \frac{1}{b}\sum_{k=1}^{b/2} k\cdot p(k,b) = \frac{12\cdot 2^b - (3b+2)2^{b/2} - 2b - 4}{6b\cdot 2^b} \xrightarrow[b\to\infty]{} \frac{2}{b} \quad (8.3.6)$$

$$\sigma_e^2 = \sum_{k=1}^{b/2} k^2\cdot p(k,b) - \left(b\omega(b)\right)^2$$

$$= 2 - \frac{3b^2 + 24b + 20}{12\cdot 2^{b/2}} + \frac{(6b+4)2^{b/2} - b^2 - 4}{6\cdot 2^b}$$
(8.3.7)

$$+ \left(\frac{(3b+2)2^{b/2} + 2b + 4}{3\cdot 2^b}\right)^2 \xrightarrow[b\to\infty]{} 2$$

Higher moments of $p(k,b)$ are useful for analyzing the spread of the BER fluctuations. Specifically, the variance of the bit error rate ε in a QAM channel is determined as follows:

$$\Sigma^2 = \frac{\left\langle \left(\xi_1\xi_2 - \langle\xi_1\xi_2\rangle\right)^2\right\rangle}{b^2} \quad (8.3.8)$$

where ξ_1 is the random variable that is equal to 1 with probability of p_{QAM} and to 0 with probability of $1 - p_{QAM}$; and p_{QAM} is defined by Equation 8.3.2; ξ_2 is the random variable that is equal to $\{1, ..., N\}$ with probabilities $\{p(1,b), ..., p(N,b)\}$. As ξ_1 and ξ_2 are independent, Equation 8.3.8 can be rewritten as:

$$\Sigma^2 = \frac{\left(\langle \xi_1^2 \rangle \langle \xi_2^2 \rangle - \langle \xi_1 \rangle^2 \langle \xi_2 \rangle^2\right)}{b^2}$$

$$= \frac{p_{QAM}\left(1 - p_{QAM}\right)\langle n_e^2 \rangle + p_{QAM}^2 \sigma_e^2}{b^2} \qquad (8.3.9)$$

where σ_e^2 is defined in Equation 8.3.7. As the BER is defined as $\varepsilon = p_{QAM}\langle n_e \rangle / b$,

$$\Sigma^2 = \Sigma_{dm}^2 + \Sigma_{ce}^2, \Sigma_{dm}^2 = \frac{\langle n_e^2 \rangle \varepsilon}{\langle n_e \rangle b}\left(1 - \frac{b\varepsilon}{\langle n_e \rangle}\right), \quad \Sigma_{ce}^2 = \frac{\sigma_e^2}{\langle n_e \rangle^2}\varepsilon^2 \quad (8.3.10)$$

At $\varepsilon \ll 1$, the demodulation part of variance dominates the constellation encoder part and:

$$\Sigma^2 \approx \frac{\langle n_e^2 \rangle \varepsilon}{\langle n_e \rangle b} \qquad (8.3.11)$$

As an example, assuming $\varepsilon = 10^{-7}$ and b = 15 [3] yields $\Sigma = 1.4 \times 10^{-4}$.

The constellation labeling used in ADSL is not Hamming-distance optimal if one compares it with the Gray labeling [5]. An example of four-bit Gray-coded constellation is shown in Figure 8.1e; in that case the Hamming-distance d_H between the nearest neighbors is always 1, $\omega(b) = 1/b$, and $\sigma_e = 0$. The benefit of the ADSL QAM constellations is that, algorithmically, they do not require lookup tables.

8.4 Nonsquare Constellations: An Asymptotic Analysis

The method of estimating error control parameters developed for square ADSL QAM constellations may be extended to the case of nonsquare constellations. A nonsquare (odd-bit) QAM constellation can be represented as a set of adjacent square subconstellations of different sizes, thus reducing the problem to the basic (even-bit) case considered in the preceding text. Figure 8.2b presents the upper left quarter of the 32-point ADSL QAM constellation. The whole constellation can be described as a 16-point QAM subconstellation shown in Figure 8.1a, with 16 adjacent points all over the perimeter of the 16-point QAM constellation. The next odd-bit constellation, 128-point QAM, is generated from this one following the rule shown in Figure 8.1c, and so on. Thus, larger constellations consist of one central 2^{2N}-point QAM subconstellation and 16 adjacent 2^{2N-4}-point QAM subconstellations.

For a general QAM constellation encoder, the probability of having k bit errors in an erroneous QAM symbol is:

$$
\begin{aligned}
p\left(k, b_1, \ldots, b_J\right) = & \sum_{j=1}^{J} \frac{2^{b_j}}{2^b} p\left(k \left| \begin{array}{c} \text{symbol transmitted } \in \Omega_j \text{ and} \\ \text{symbol received } \in \Omega_j \end{array} \right.\right) \\
& + \sum_{j,m\,(m \ne j)}^{J} \left[p\left(\begin{array}{c} \text{symbol transmitted } \in \Omega_j \text{ and} \\ \text{symbol received } \in \Omega_m \end{array} \right) \right. \\
& \left. \times p\left(k \left| \begin{array}{c} \text{symbol transmitted } \in \Omega_j \text{ and} \\ \text{symbol received } \in \Omega_m \end{array} \right.\right) \right]
\end{aligned}
\tag{8.4.1}
$$

where 2^{b_j} is the number of constellation points in each of J adjacent square subconstellations Ω_j forming the nonsquare constellation considered; and the following condition holds:

$$
\sum_{j=1}^{J} \frac{2^{b_j}}{2^b} = 1
\tag{8.4.2}
$$

The Hamming distance between two neighbor points belonging to the same 2^{b_j}-point square subconstellation cannot be larger than $b_j/2 \le b/2$. However, if two neighbor points of the constellation belong to different adjacent subconstellations, their d_H can exceed $b/2$. For instance, d_H between the points labeled by 9 and 19 in Figure 8.2b equals 3.

As evaluating $p(k, b_1, \ldots, b_J)$ from Equation 8.4.1 in each specific case of a nonsquare constellation is cumbersome, the following general result can be derived:

Proposition 3

Let a nonsquare 2^b-point QAM constellation consist of J adjacent square subconstellations. Let each 2^{b_j}-point subconstellation have been generated recursively according to the rule shown in Figure 8.1c. Denote

$$b_* = \min b_j, \ j = 1, \ \ldots, \ J$$

Then at large b_j, $j = 1, \ldots, J$, and at $1 \leq k \leq b_*/2$, $p(k, b_1, \ldots, b_J)$ becomes asymptotically close to $p(k,b)$, the error probability function given by Equation 8.3.5:

$$p(k, b_1, \ldots, b_j) \to p(k, b), \text{ as } b_j \to \infty, j = 1, \ldots, J$$

Proof Consider the different terms in Equation 8.4.1. To determine the conditional probability in the first sum on the right-hand side of Equation 8.4.1, one has to use Equation 8.3.5 at $1 \leq k \leq b_*/2$, for each subconstellation. Generally, this conditional probability has to be complemented by a correction term. This correction term accounts for the change in cardinality of some external points of a square b_j-bit subconstellation as a result of bringing it in contact with another subconstellation. For instance, a point with the value of 11 in Figure 8.2b has the cardinality of 3 in a stand-alone square 16-point QAM constellation; but its cardinality is 4 as a part of the 32-point QAM constellation. The ratio of this correction term to the value given by Equation 8.3.5 is of the order of the ratio of the perimeter of a $2^{b_j/2} \times 2^{b_j/2}$ square to its area:

$$\text{Correction term} \sim \frac{2^{\frac{b_j}{2}}}{2^{b_j}} = 2^{\frac{-b_j}{2}} \to 0, \text{ as } b_j \to \infty$$

Similarly, under the nearest-neighbor-error supposition, the first probability of the product in the second sum on the right-hand side of Equation 8.4.1 is of the order of the ratio of the perimeter of a $2^{b_j/2} \times 2^{b_j/2}$ square to the total number of constellation points 2^b, i.e., $\sim 2^{b_j/2}/2^b$. The second (conditional) probability is, again, of the order of the ratio of the perimeter of a $2^{b_j/2} \times 2^{b_j/2}$ square to its area, i.e., $\sim 2^{-b_j/2}$. Evaluating the whole expression in Equation 8.4.1 at large b_j, $j = 1, \ldots, J$, yields:

$$p\left(k,b_1,...,b_J\right) = \sum_{j=1}^{J} \frac{2^{b_j}}{2^b}\frac{1}{2^k}\left[1 + O\left(\frac{1}{2^{\frac{b_j}{2}}}\right)\right] + O\left(\frac{1}{2^b}\right) \quad (8.4.3)$$

As $1 \leq k \leq b_*/2$ and $b_j < b$, $j = 1, ..., J$, applying Equation 8.4.2 to Equation 8.4.3 yields:

$$p\left(k,b_1,..,b_J\right) = \frac{1}{2^k}\sum_{j=1}^{J}\frac{2^{b_j}}{2^b} + \frac{1}{2^k}\sum_{j=1}^{J}\frac{2^{b_j}}{2^b}O\left(\frac{1}{2^{\frac{b_j}{2}}}\right) + \frac{1}{2^k}O\left(\frac{2^k}{2^b}\right)$$

$$ = \frac{1}{2^k}\left[1 + O\left(\frac{1}{2^{\frac{b}{2}}}\right)\right] \quad (8.4.4)$$

Finally, combining Equation 8.3.5 and Equation 8.4.4 yields:

$$p\left(k,b_1,...,b_J\right) = \frac{1}{2^k}\left[1 + O\left(\frac{1}{2^{\frac{b}{2}}}\right)\right] = p\left(k,b\right)\left[1 + O\left(\frac{1}{2^{\frac{b}{2}}}\right)\right] \quad (8.4.5)$$

Proposition 3 forms a basis for approximating the $p(k,b_1, ..., b_J)$ moments of odd-bit constellation encoders by equations developed above for even-bit constellations. Because the series for determining moments (e.g., Equation 8.3.1 or Equation 8.4.1) are convergent, the contribution of the $p(k,b_1, ..., b_J)$ "tail" at $k > b_*/2$ to these moments becomes negligible, as the subconstellation sizes grow. Thus, asymptotically, the moments of odd-bit ADSL QAM encoders depend on b only.

8.5 Comparison with Numerical Simulations

Table 8.1 shows the $\omega(b)$ values found from Equation 8.3.6 and those determined from MatLab simulations of an ADSL QAM channel. One can see that our analytical results are in an excellent agreement with channel simulations. At even b, both sets of results are pretty close in the entire range of b; at odd b, the difference between analytical results and simulations decreases as b increases.

Table 8.1   Comparison of ω(b) Values Found from Equation 8.3.6 and Determined from Numerical Simulations

b	ω(b), Equation 8.3.6	ω(b), Simulations
2	5.000000E-001	5.000000E-001
3	3.812173E-001	5.157002E-001
4	3.229167E-001	3.394366E-001
5	2.852432E-001	3.601190E-001
6	2.569444E-001	2.538012E-001
7	2.339629E-001	2.674897E-001
8	2.145182E-001	2.164009E-001
9	1.976926E-001	1.964286E-001
10	1.829427E-001	1.848450E-001
11	1.699077E-001	1.566952E-001
12	1.583252E-001	1.688679E-001
13	1.479916E-001	1.499222E-001
14	1.387416E-001	1.389728E-001
15	1.304369E-001	1.322208E-001

Although Equation 8.3.6 is expected to be a good approximation of ω(b) at large, odd b values, there is a substantial deviation between Equation 8.3.6 and numerical simulations at small, odd b values, e.g., b = 3 and b = 5. Note that as the five-bit constellation is a base for recursive generation of larger odd-bit constellations, its probabilistic properties are not expected to comply with the asymptotic equation (Equation 8.4.5). The three-bit case is an exception [3], and it stands apart from other constellations. For these values, one has to apply Equation 8.3.1, which drastically improves the agreement with numerical simulations (see Table 8.2).

One should note that the BER is sometimes taken to be equal to the QAM symbol error rate (or ω = 1; see, for example, [6], p. 15). As our results show, this assumption is not justified and, for large QAM constellations, may misevaluate BER by one order (which may save about 0.5 dB on the margin).

Table 8.2 Comparison of ω(b) Values Found from Equation 8.3.1 and Determined from Numerical Simulations at b < 7

b	ω(b), Equation 8.3.1	ω(b), Simulations
2	0.5	0.5
3	0.528	0.516
4	0.323	0.339
5	0.358	0.360
6	0.256	0.254

8.6 Conclusions

To summarize, an analytical method of estimating the BER of ADSL QAM constellation encoders is developed in this chapter. This method uses constellations self-similarity with respect to the distribution of the Hamming distance between the nearest neighbors. The probability of having m bit errors in an erroneous b-bit QAM symbol is derived. The average fraction of erroneous bits in an erroneous QAM symbol is found to be inversely proportional to b/2 at large b. The standard deviation of the number of bit errors in an erroneous QAM symbol is derived and used for analyzing the spread of the BER fluctuations.

The method developed for square constellations is extended to nonsquare constellations. It is shown that at large b, the equations describing probabilistic properties of odd-bit constellation encoders are the same that were derived in the even-bit case.

References

1. Chen, W.Y., *DSL: Simulation Techniques and Standards Development for Digital Subscriber Line Systems*, Indianapolis: Macmillan Technical Publishing, 1998.
2. Proakis, J., *Digital Communications*, New York: McGraw-Hill, 1995.
3. *ITU Recommendation G.992.2: Splitterless Asymmetric Digital Subscriber Line (ADSL) Transceivers*, Geneva, 1999.
4. Mandelbrot, B.B., *The Fractal Geometry of Nature*, San Francisco: Freeman, 1982.
5. Simon, M.K., Hinedi, S.M., and Lindsey, W.C., *Digital Communication Techniques*, New York: Prentice Hall, 1995.
6. Chow, P.S., Bandwidth Optimized Digital Transmission Techniques for Spectrally Shaped Channels with Impulse Noise, Ph.D. thesis, Stanford University, May 1993.

Chapter 9

Throughput Optimization in a General Duplex Communications System with FEC and ARQ

9.1 Background

In this chapter, an exact solution for the throughput of a general duplex communications system with forward error correction (FEC) and automatic repeat request (ARQ) is constructed. A graphical representation of this solution relating the channel throughputs in both the upstream and downstream directions is developed. The chapter is organized as follows. First, a nomenclature to fully describe a duplex communications system using FEC and ARQ is established. Then some fundamental properties of such a system are derived and used to formulate the equations for the joint optimization of throughput in both directions.

9.2 A System Model with FEC and ARQ

Consider a duplex data transmission between two stations in which both upstream and downstream stations send information and acknowledgment frames. The error-controlling algorithm uses a combination of an FEC code and a cyclic redundancy check (CRC). The forward error correction can be any type of code but we will consider Reed–Solomon (RS) codes here. Each information frame has a length of N code symbols containing an information field of length K symbols. The N–K redundant code symbols are divided into a CRC field of length C symbols and a parity check field of length R symbols, i.e., N = K + C + R. The number of correctable symbol errors, t, depends on R. Each acknowledgment frame is of length M code symbols and M << N. The line data rate (the rate at which all user and redundant bits flow), in bits per second, is V. To optimize the system for a particular application, it is likely that upstream/downstream requirements will be different. When both directions are considered simultaneously, we will differentiate the parameters used in upstream/downstream directions by adding a "u" or a "d" subscript, respectively.

The t-error correcting is assumed to correct all information frames that are received with no more than t errors. Also, for any frame with more than t errors, the CRC is assumed to always detect the residual errors after FEC. In this case, a negative acknowledgment frame will be sent to the peer, and the frame will be retransmitted. A limit of k is imposed on the number of frame transmissions (k = 1 indicates that no retransmissions will take place). A positive acknowledgment is sent to the peer for every m information frames correctly received. Our other simplifying assumptions are that no packets are lost in transmission and that all acknowledgment frames are received correctly.

The communications system considered is shown in Figure 9.1a as a circuit. The calculation of information flows in this circuit will be performed using the theory of queuing networks; therefore, we will denote the information transfer rate as intensity. The input intensities (in frames/sec) of the information to be transferred are application dependent and denoted by λ_{in}. Control symbols are added to each frame before the information is sent. The total transmitter intensities in the upstream/downstream direction are given as $\lambda_t = \lambda_{ti} + \lambda_{ta}$, where λ_{ti} is the intensity of information frames and λ_{ta} is the intensity of acknowledgment frames. The upstream/downstream station receives an information frame and determines if it is correctable. The intensity of correctable frames is denoted as λ_{pout}. For each noncorrectable information frame, the upstream/downstream station sends a negative

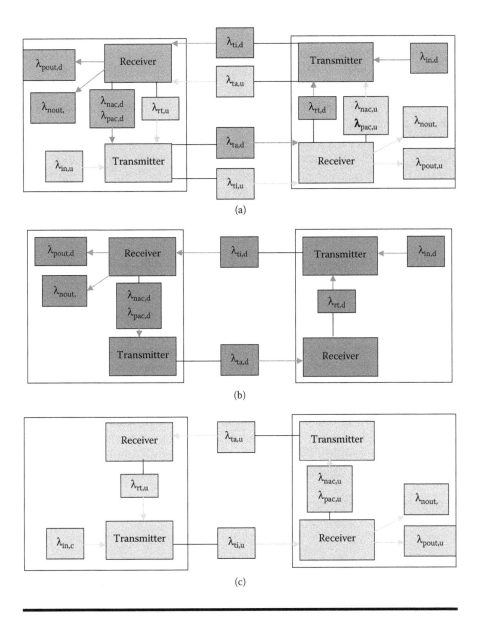

Figure 9.1 **The communication circuit considered (a) can be viewed as a superposition of two simpler circuits (b) and (c).**

acknowledgment. The intensity of these negative acknowledgment frames is denoted by λ_{nac}. The intensity of retransmissions sent in response to the negative acknowledgments is denoted by λ_{rt}. When an information frame has been transmitted k times and still has errors, it is allowed to pass to the output stream with the intensity of λ_{nout}. The intensity of positive acknowledgments sent from the upstream/downstream station for every m correctable information frames is denoted as λ_{pac}. Clearly, the following equality holds: $\lambda_{ta} = \lambda_{nac} + \lambda_{pac}$.

All of these intensities may be different in the upstream and downstream directions. We will differentiate the direction of the intensities by adding a "u" or "d" subscript to those associated with information flowing in the upstream or downstream direction, respectively. This means that acknowledgment frames associated with information flowing in the upstream direction will be given a "u" subscript even though those frames flow in the downstream direction.

9.3 Joint Optimization of FEC and ARQ Parameters in Both Directions

This method of allocating the subscripts allows us to split the model into two circuits shown in Figure 9.1b and Figure 9.1c. Both circuits transmit only data frames in one direction and only acknowledgment frames in the other direction, and each has consistent subscripts. The "data downstream–acknowledgment upstream" and "data upstream–acknowledgment downstream" circuits are shown in Figure 9.1b and Figure 9.1c, respectively. Let us consider the circuit shown in Figure 9.1b.

The channel introduces an error with the channel symbol error rate of p_e. The probability p of an information frame being accepted in this scheme (i.e., having t or less symbols in error) is:

$$p = \sum_{i=0}^{t} p_e^i \left(1 - p_e\right)^{N-i} \binom{N}{i} \tag{9.3.1}$$

t can be calculated from R as follows. If e_r positions of unreliable code symbols (erasures) are made known to the decoder, the number of errors corrected by an RS code with redundancy R is

$$t = \left\lfloor \frac{\left(R + 1 + e_r\right)}{2} \right\rfloor, \tag{9.3.2}$$

where the maximum of errors corrected is R and this is reached when $e_r = R$.

Considering the flow of acknowledgments in the channel, one has:

$$\lambda_{rt} = \lambda_{nac} \frac{(1-p)+(1-p)^2+\ldots+(1-p)^{k-1}}{(1-p)+(1-p)^2+\ldots+(1-p)^{k-1}+(1-p)^k} \tag{9.3.3}$$

$$= \lambda_{nac}\left[1-(1-p)^{k-1}\right]\Big/\left[1-(1-p)^k\right]$$

$$\lambda_{nout} = \lambda_{nac} \frac{(1-p)^k}{(1-p)+(1-p)^2+\ldots+(1-p)^{k-1}+(1-p)^k}$$

$$= \frac{\lambda_{nac}p(1-p)^{k-1}}{\left[1-(1-p)^k\right]} \tag{9.3.4}$$

and $\lambda_{nac} = \lambda_{rt} + \lambda_{nout}$. Equation 9.3.3 and Equation 9.3.4 imply that the probability of an information frame being uncorrectable at the receiver and having been transmitted <k times is just:

$$\frac{1-(1-p)^{k-1}}{1-(1-p)^k},$$

and, upon receiving this frame, the downstream station sends a negative acknowledgment.

At the upstream station, $\lambda_{ti} = \lambda_{in} + \lambda_{rt}$, or

$$\lambda_{ti} = \lambda_{in} + \frac{\lambda_{nac}\left[1-(1-p)^{k-1}\right]}{\left[1-(1-p)^k\right]} \tag{9.3.5}$$

as the information flow in the downstream direction consists of new frames and retransmissions.

At the downstream receiver, the input is divided into correctable (with probability p) and uncorrectable (with probability 1 − p) frames. This yields:

$$\lambda_{pout} = p\lambda_{ti} = p\lambda_{in} + \frac{\lambda_{nac}p\left[1-(1-p)^{k-1}\right]}{\left[1-(1-p)^k\right]} \tag{9.3.6}$$

and, as an uncorrectable frame, transmitted less than k times, generates one negative acknowledgment,

$$\lambda_{nac} = (1 - p)\lambda_{ti} \tag{9.3.7}$$

Combining Equation 9.3.7 and Equation 9.3.5 yields an equation for determining λ_{nac}:

$$\lambda_{nac} = (1 - p)\lambda_{in} + \frac{\lambda_{nac}(1 - p)\left[1 - (1 - p)^{k-1}\right]}{\left[1 - (1 - p)^{k}\right]} \tag{9.3.8}$$

which yields:

$$\lambda_{nac} = \frac{\lambda_{in}\left[1 - (1 - p)^{k}\right](1 - p)}{p} \tag{9.3.9}$$

Now, one can express all other intensities defined earlier, in terms of λ_{in}:

$$\lambda_{ti} = \frac{\lambda_{in}\left[1 - (1 - p)^{k}\right]}{p}, \tag{9.3.10}$$

$$\lambda_{pout} = \lambda_{in}\left[1 - (1 - p)^{k}\right], \tag{9.3.11}$$

$$\lambda_{rt} = \frac{\lambda_{in}(1 - p)\left[1 - (1 - p)^{k-1}\right]}{p}, \tag{9.3.12}$$

$$\lambda_{nout} = \lambda_{in}(1 - p)^{k} \tag{9.3.13}$$

$$\lambda_{pac} = \frac{p\lambda_{ti}}{m} = \frac{\lambda_{in}\left[1 - (1 - p)^{k}\right]}{m} \tag{9.3.14}$$

$$\lambda_{ta} = \lambda_{in}\left[\frac{1}{m} + \frac{1-p}{p}\right]\left[1 - (1-p)^k\right] \qquad (9.3.15)$$

Note that Equation 9.3.11 and Equation 9.3.13 show the expected result that the number of information bits sent by the upstream application, Λ, per unit time is equal to the information input intensity:

$$\Lambda = \alpha K(\lambda_{pout} + \lambda_{nout}) = \alpha K \lambda_{in} \qquad (9.3.16)$$

where α is the number of bits in each RS code symbol. We call Λ the net data rate to differentiate it from the line data rate, V, which includes all of the bits that are transmitted. The derivation for the circuit shown in Figure 9.1c is identical. This means that using the appropriate subscripts, intensities in the circuit shown in Figure 9.1a have been determined.

The preceding derivation assumes arbitrary values of λ_{in} in both directions. In a real system, there are two upper bounds on $\lambda_{in,u}$ and $\lambda_{in,d}$ related to the line data rates, V_u and V_d:

$$\alpha N_u \lambda_{ti,u} + \alpha M_d \lambda_{ta,d} \leq V_u \qquad (9.3.17)$$

$$\alpha N_d \lambda_{ti,d} + \alpha M_u \lambda_{ta,u} \leq V_d \qquad (9.3.18)$$

Applying Equation 9.3.10, Equation 9.3.15, and Equation 9.3.16 to inequalities given by Equation 9.3.17 and Equation 9.3.18 yields:

$$\frac{M_d}{K_d}\left[\frac{1}{m_d} + \frac{1-p_d}{p_d}\right]\left[1-(1-p_d)^{k_d}\right]\Lambda_d + \frac{N_u}{K_u}\frac{1-(1-p_u)^{k_u}}{p_u}\Lambda_u \leq V_u \quad (9.3.19)$$

$$\frac{M_u}{K_u}\left[\frac{1}{m_u} + \frac{1-p_u}{p_u}\right]\left[1-(1-p_u)^{k_u}\right]\Lambda_u + \frac{N_d}{K_d}\frac{1-(1-p_d)^{k_d}}{p_d}\Lambda_d \leq V_d \quad (9.3.20)$$

The ultimate goal in designing a communications system should be to jointly maximize its throughput, H, in the upstream/downstream directions, i.e., to find $H_u = \max \Lambda_u$ and $H_d = \max \Lambda_d$. In a scheme with retransmissions, the throughputs cannot be maximized independently

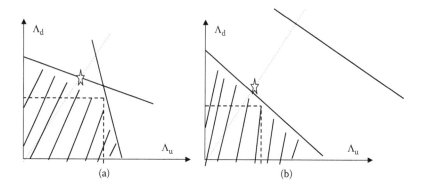

Figure 9.2 Possible solutions (the shaded regions) of Equation 9.3.19, Equation 9.3.20 (the bold lines), and Equation 9.3.21 (the dotted lines). The * symbol represents the optimum. The dashed lines illustrate the relationship between the channel throughput values in the upstream and downstream directions.

because the transmission in one direction uses some of the data transfer capacity in the other direction. One has to choose Λ_d and maximize Λ_u by applying the constraints given by Equation 9.3.19 and Equation 9.3.20. This procedure allows one to relate the throughput values of the upstream and downstream channels, as shown in Figure 9.2a and Figure 9.2b.

To jointly optimize the throughputs, it is necessary to allocate a partitioning of the available channel capacity to each transfer direction. The condition used here will be equating Λ_u/Λ_d to ξ, i.e.:

$$H = \max (\Lambda_u + \Lambda_d) = H_u + H_d, \text{ as } \Lambda_u = \xi\Lambda_d, \qquad (9.3.21)$$

The bandwidth distribution ratio, ξ, is ~0.1 for Internet browsing, ~0 for file downloads, and ~0.5 for peer-to-peer communications. By drawing straight lines bounding the solution regions of Equation 9.3.19 and Equation 9.3.20 in the (Λ_u, Λ_d) plane, the optimization can be seen graphically. Depending on whether the two straight lines intersect inside or outside the first quadrant of the (Λ_u, Λ_d) plane, one has the situations shown in Figure 9.2a and Figure 9.2b. In both cases, the solution of Equation 9.3.19 to Equation 9.3.21 corresponds to the intersection of a straight line given by Equation 9.3.21 and one of the solution boundaries of Equation 9.3.19 or Equation 9.3.20. The optimum is dependent on which restriction, Equation 9.3.19 or Equation 9.3.20, is stronger. In Figure 9.2a, in which the solution boundaries cross, which restriction is stronger depends on ξ.

The graphical solution of Equation 9.3.19 to Equation 9.3.21 may be presented in the analytical form:

$$H_d = \max \Lambda_d = \min \left\{ \begin{array}{l} V_d \left/ \left[\dfrac{N_d}{K_d} \dfrac{1-(1-p_d)^{k_d}}{p_d} + \dfrac{M_u}{K_u} \xi \left(\dfrac{1}{m_u} + \dfrac{1-p_u}{p_u} \right) \left(1-(1-p_d)^{k_d} \right) \right], \right. \\[2em] V_u \left/ \left[\dfrac{M_d}{K_d} \left(\dfrac{1}{m_d} + \dfrac{1-p_d}{p_d} \right) \left(1-(1-p_d)^{k_d} \right) + \xi \dfrac{N_u}{K_u} \dfrac{1-(1-p_u)^{k_u}}{p_u} \right] \right. \end{array} \right\} \quad (9.3.22)$$

$$H_u = \max \Lambda_u = \min \left\{ \begin{array}{l} \xi V_d \left/ \left[\dfrac{N_d}{K_d} \dfrac{1-(1-p_d)^{k_d}}{p_d} + \dfrac{M_u}{K_u} \xi \left(\dfrac{1}{m_u} + \dfrac{1-p_u}{p_u} \right) \left(1-(1-p_u)^{k_u} \right) \right], \right. \\[2em] \xi V_u \left/ \left[\dfrac{M_d}{K_d} \left(\dfrac{1}{m_d} + \dfrac{1-p_d}{p_d} \right) \left(1-(1-p_d)^{k_d} \right) + \xi \dfrac{N_u}{K_u} \dfrac{1-(1-p_u)^{k_u}}{p_u} \right] \right. \end{array} \right\} \quad (9.3.23)$$

9.4 Conclusions

The results of this chapter allow the joint optimization, for a given ξ, of the upstream and downstream throughput in a general duplex channel with FEC and ARQ.

References

1. Proakis, J.G., *Digital Communications,* New York: McGraw-Hill, 1995.
2. Bertsekas, D. and Gallager, R., *Data Networks,* Upper Saddle River, NJ: Prentice Hall, 1992.
3. Mitlin, V., Williams, R.G.C., Performance Evaluation of Multicarrier Channels with Forward Error Correction and Automatic Repeat Request. U.S. Patent No. 20020108081, 2002.
4. Mitlin, V. and Williams, R.G.C., Performance Evaluation of Multicarrier Channels, U.S. Patent No. 20030105997, 2003.

Chapter 10

A Quantitative Procedure of Optimizing the MAC Packet Size in TCP/IP-Compliant Networks

10.1 Background

Consider a TCP/IP session optimization problem in networks in which each MAC packet is transmitted completely over one link before starting transmission to the next. Following Bertsekas and Gallager [1], such networks will be called *cut-through routing-free* networks or *CTRF networks*. Examples of CTRF networks are those compliant with IEEE 802.11 wireless LAN [2] or IEEE 802.16 wireless MAN [3] standards. Contrarily, a typical wire line network (for instance, IEEE-802.3-compliant one) is a *cut-through routing* (CTR) kind of network. In CTR networks, a node starts relaying any portion of a packet to another node without waiting to receive the packet in its entirety. The nature of CTR in CTR networks is such that error detection and retransmission cannot be done on a node-to-node basis; it has to be done on an end-to-end basis [1]. That is the main reason why wireless networks, which are more prone to channel noise than wire line networks, are standardized as CTRF networks. This allows not only for TCP/IP layer (end-to-end) but also media access layer (node-to-node) error control. This chapter presents an analytical method of optimal breaking of a TCP/IP message into MAC packets in networks without CTR (such as networks compliant with the IEEE 802.11 wireless LAN standard). The method accounts for the transmission delay of acknowledgment frames, the sliding window flow control in TCP/IP protocol, error control via retransmissions, and heterogeneity of transport parameters (link-to-link and upstream/downstream) along a multihop network path. Mathematically, the problem consists of minimizing the TCP/IP message transaction time, a nonlinear function of the MAC packet size, in the presence of a set of linear restrictions. Throughput calculations illustrating this method are performed using IEEE 802.11 data.

The following terminology will be used throughout this chapter: a network consists of *nodes* or *stations*; *links* connect the nodes; and a *packet* transmitted over a link makes a *hop*.

10.2 Statement of the Problem of Optimizing the MAC Packet Size in TCP/IP-Compliant Networks

In a TCP/IP session, each TCP/IP message is broken into MAC packets that are then transmitted over the network path. Let each MAC packet be framed such that each MAC frame contains a fixed number V of overhead bits (i.e., frame header and trailer). Let K denote the length of a MAC packet. One has a distribution of TCP/IP message lengths, and each message is broken into as many packets of size K as possible, with the last packet containing the leftover. A TCP/IP message of length M would be broken into $\lceil M/K \rceil$ packets, where $\lceil \ \rceil$ is the smallest integer greater than or equal to a given real number. The first $\lceil M/K \rceil - 1$ packets each contain K bits, and the final packet contains between 1 and K bits. The total number of bits in the resulting frames is ([1], p.93):

$$\text{Total bits} = M + \left\lceil \frac{M}{K} \right\rceil \cdot V \qquad (10.2.1)$$

One can see from Equation 10.2.1 that as K decreases, the number of frames and, thus, the total overhead in the TCP/IP message, $\lceil M/K \rceil \times V$, increases. This speaks in favor of transmitting larger MAC frames. Each link must perform a certain amount of processing per frame; as K decreases, the number of frames and, thus, the processing load, increases. In other words, both transmission and processing overheads favor large K values.

The pipelining effect [1] is the factor that favors small values of K. Namely, let the packets arrive to each link in the same order they were transmitted. If the entire TCP/IP message is sent as one packet, the total message transaction time in the network is the sum of the message transmission times for each link. If the TCP/IP message is broken into several packets, the earlier packets may proceed along the path while the source node is transmitting the latter packets, thus reducing the message transaction time.

In a CTRF network, the combined effect of overhead and pipelining on the TCP/IP message transaction time can be described as the following generalization of approach [1]. Let a TCP/IP message of length M be broken into MAC packets, with a final packet of typically shorter length. The message must be transmitted over J links (i.e., from the source, 0-th node to the destination, J-th node on the (J + 1)-node network path). In a TCP/IP session, each MAC packet arriving at the destination has to be acknowledgd by sending a short acknowledgment packet of length A back to the source node. No more than N MAC packets are transmitted from the source node until acknowledgments from previously sent MAC packets arrive. This is called the *window flow control* [1], with the size of the window (or the number of outstanding frames) being equal to N. Finally, a request of X bits is sent from the destination before transmitting the TCP/IP message, and a reply of Y bits is sent from the source after transmitting the message.

The total transaction time T required to transmit the TCP/IP message from the source to the destination is a sum of several terms. First, it is the time needed for the first MAC packet to travel over the first J − 1 links. Next, the time it takes for the entire TCP/IP message to travel over the final link ([1], p. 94) is added. Possible delays related to the window flow control are added next. Finally, the time needed to transmit the TCP/IP message request and reply between the source and destination is added. The result is:

$$T = (K + V) \sum_{j=1}^{J-1} \tau_{j,d} + \left(M + \left\lceil \frac{M}{K} \right\rceil \cdot V \right) \tau_{J,d}$$

$$+ \left\lfloor \frac{\lceil M/K \rceil}{N} \right\rfloor \cdot E(K) \cdot h(E(K)) + X \sum_{j=1}^{J} \tau_{j,u} + Y \sum_{j=1}^{J} \tau_{j,d}$$

(10.2.2)

where $\lfloor\ \rfloor$ is the largest integer smaller than or equal to a given real number; h(…) is the Heaviside unit step function (1 at positive argument, 0 otherwise);

$$E(K) = (K+V)\sum_{j=1}^{J}\tau_{j,d} + A\sum_{j=1}^{J}\tau_{j,u} - N(K + V)\tau_{1,d} \qquad (10.2.3)$$

τ_j is an average delay per bit at the link j that, for moderate-to-heavy network loads, can be defined using the Kleinrock approximation ([4]; [1], p.211):

$$\tau_j = \frac{1}{\mu_j - \lambda_j} + w_j \qquad (10.2.4)$$

λ_j is the total arrival rate to link j (in bits per second); μ_j is the average transmission rate on link j (in bits per second); and w_j is the average processing (e.g., encryption, compression, etc.) delay on link j (in seconds per bit). The d and u subscripts in Equation 10.2.2 indicate the downstream and upstream transmission directions, respectively. As a TCP/IP session is considered, the media access layer details are hidden in the integral quantity τ_j, and are not discussed here. Also, it is assumed that both acknowledgment and information frames go through the same processing cycle on each link.

Figure 10.1 illustrates Equation 10.2.2. Basically, there are two possible scenarios. The first scenario is abbreviated ASW (i.e., acknowledgments arrive at the source node slower than the window slides). Here, as shown in Figure 10.1b, an additional delay equal to the sum of the total transmission time of one MAC frame sent downstream and the total transmission time of one acknowledgment frame sent upstream discounted by the total transmission time in the window (Equation 10.2.3) should be accounted for each N packets in T. That is why the term ~Eh(E) appears in Equation 10.2.2. The $\lfloor\lceil M/K\rceil/N\rfloor$ term is the number of these additional delays per TCP/IP message. The second scenario is abbreviated AFW (i.e., acknowledgments arrive to the source node faster than the window slides). Here, as shown in Figure 10.1a, no additional delay has to be accounted for in the expression for T.

Let us average Equation 10.2.2 over the M distribution. If this distribution is reasonably uniform over spans of K bits, the following equality holds [1]:

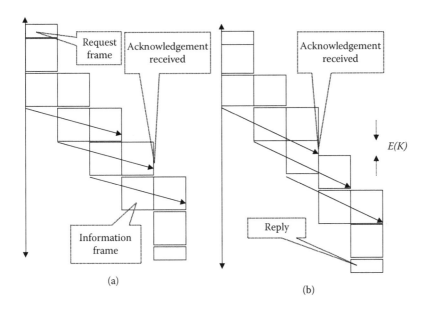

Figure 10.1 **Sketch of the pipelining effect. A TCP/IP message is broken into five packets and transmitted over two links as MAC frames. Two-sided arrows show the total message transmission time. One-sided arrows show the acknowledgments sent, and three outstanding frames are transmitted in the window. (a) the AFW scenario, (b) the ASW scenario.**

$$\left\langle \left[\frac{M}{K} \right] \right\rangle = \left\langle \frac{M}{K} \right\rangle + 0.5 = \frac{\langle M \rangle}{K} + 0.5 \qquad (10.2.5)$$

Analogously, one can show (see Section 10.3) that:

$$\left\langle \left[\frac{\left[\frac{M}{K} \right]}{N} \right] \right\rangle = \frac{\langle M \rangle}{KN} - 0.5 \qquad (10.2.6)$$

Then, the average TCP/IP message transaction time is:

$$\langle T \rangle = \langle K + V \rangle \sum_{j=1}^{J-1} \tau_{j,d} + \left(\langle M \rangle + \frac{\langle M \rangle}{K} V + \frac{V}{2} \right) \tau_{J,d}$$

$$+ \left(\frac{\langle M \rangle}{KN} - 0.5 \right) E(K) \cdot h(E(K)) + X \sum_{j=1}^{J} \tau_{j,u} + Y \sum_{j=1}^{J} \tau_{j,d} \qquad (10.2.7)$$

For networks with homogeneous parameters, Equation 10.2.7 will simplify as follows:

$$\frac{\langle T \rangle}{\tau} = (K + V)(J - 1) + \left(\langle M \rangle + \frac{\langle M \rangle}{K} V + \frac{V}{2} \right)$$

$$+ \left(\frac{\langle M \rangle}{KN} - 0.5 \right) E(K) \cdot h(E(K)) + (X + Y) J \qquad (10.2.8)$$

where t is an average delay per bit at a link. Our goal is to find the optimum K by minimizing $\langle T \rangle$ in Equation 10.2.7 or Equation 10.2.8. A natural restriction for the optimum solution is:

$$0 < K \leq \langle M \rangle \qquad (10.2.9)$$

The problem is more complex than the one considered in [1], as $\langle T \rangle$ is a nonlinear function of K with discontinuous derivative. Its solution is presented in Section 10.5.

For a relatively narrow distribution of TCP/IP message lengths, the throughput R is estimated as follows:

$$R = \frac{\langle M \rangle}{\langle T \rangle} \qquad (10.2.10)$$

i.e., minimizing the TCP/IP message transaction time is equivalent to maximizing the throughput. Generally, M/T weighted with the probability density of the M distribution should be integrated over M to obtain the throughput.

10.3 Derivation of Equation 10.2.6

Let:

$$M = aK + b \qquad (10.3.1)$$

$$a = cN + d , \qquad (10.3.2)$$

and all quantities in Equation 10.3.1 and Equation 10.3.2 are nonnegative integers. Combining Equation 10.3.1 and Equation 10.3.2 yields:

$$M = cKN + dK + b \qquad (10.3.3)$$

or

$$\frac{M}{K} = cN + d + \frac{b}{K} \qquad (10.3.4)$$

As $0 \le b < K$ and $K \gg 1$, it follows from Equation 10.3.4 that for random distributions of M that are reasonably uniform over spans of K (a property used in [1]), one has:

$$\lceil M/K \rceil = cN + d + 1 \qquad (10.3.5)$$

with high probability of $(K - 1)/K$ (i.e., unless $b = 0$). Similarly, it is easy to see that:

$$\left\lfloor \frac{\lceil M/K \rceil}{N} \right\rfloor = c \qquad (10.3.6)$$

with probability of $1 - (K - 1)/KN$ (i.e., unless $d = N - 1$). Next, it follows from Equation 10.3.3 that:

$$\frac{M}{KN} = c + \left(\frac{d + b/K}{N} \right)$$

which yields:

$$\lfloor M/KN \rfloor \equiv \lceil M/KN \rceil - 1 = c \qquad (10.3.7)$$

Combining Equation 10.3.6 and Equation 10.3.7 yields, with probability of $1 - (K - 1)/KN$ at $KN \gg 1$,

$$\left\lfloor \frac{\lceil M/KN \rceil}{N} \right\rfloor = \lceil M/KN \rceil - 1 \qquad (10.3.8)$$

As a typical value of N is substantially larger than 1 (e.g., the Microsoft TCP/IP implementation default value is 8), the approximation (Equation 10.3.8) appears accurate enough.

Now, let us average Equation 10.3.8 over the M distribution. Extending the result of [1] and using Equation 10.3.8, if this distribution is reasonably uniform over spans of KN, Equation 10.2.6 is derived:

$$\left\langle \left[\frac{\left[\frac{M}{K} \right]}{N} \right] \right\rangle = \left\langle \left[\frac{M}{KN} \right] \right\rangle - 1 = \left(\frac{\langle M \rangle}{KN} - 0.5 \right)\left(1 + O\left(\frac{K-1}{KN} \right) \right) \quad (10.3.9)$$

10.4 Determining the Optimal MAC Packet Size in the Case of a Variable MAC Frame Length

To minimize $\langle T \rangle$ with respect to K, let us present Equation 10.2.7 as follows: find

$$\langle T \rangle_{min} = \min\left(\langle T \rangle_{AFW}, \langle T \rangle_{ASW} \right) \quad (10.4.1)$$

where

$$\langle T \rangle_{AFW} = \min \left\{ \begin{array}{l} \left(K + V \right) \sum_{j=1}^{J-1} \tau_{j,d} + \left(\langle M \rangle + \frac{\langle M \rangle}{K} V + \frac{V}{2} \right) \tau_{J,d} \\[2em] + X \sum_{j=1}^{J} \tau_{j,u} + Y \sum_{j=1}^{J} \tau_{j,d} \end{array} \right\} \quad (10.4.2)$$

$$\left(K + V \right) \sum_{j=1}^{J} \tau_{j,d} + A \sum_{j=1}^{J} \tau_{j,u} - N\left(K + V \right)\tau_{1,d} \le 0, \quad (10.4.3)$$

and

$$\langle T \rangle_{ASW} = \min \left\{ \begin{array}{l} \left[(K+V) \sum_{j=1}^{J-1} \tau_{j,d} + \left(\langle M \rangle + \frac{\langle M \rangle}{K} V + \frac{V}{2} \right) \tau_{J,d} \right] \\[4pt] + \left(\frac{\langle M \rangle}{KN} - 0.5 \right) \\[4pt] \times \left[(K+V) \sum_{i=1}^{J} \tau_{i,d} + A \sum_{j=1}^{J} \tau_{j,u} - N(K+V) \tau_{1,d} \right] \\[4pt] + X \sum_{j=1}^{J} \tau_{j,u} + Y \sum_{j=1}^{J} \tau_{j,d} \end{array} \right\} \tag{10.4.4}$$

$$(K+V) \sum_{j=1}^{J} \tau_{j,d} + A \sum_{j=1}^{J} \tau_{j,u} - N(K+V)\tau_{1,d} > 0 \tag{10.4.5}$$

as

$$0 < K \le \langle M \rangle \tag{10.4.6}$$

System (Equation 10.4.1) to (Equation 10.4.6) can be rewritten in an equivalent form:

$$\langle T \rangle_{min} = \min \left(\langle T \rangle_{AFW}, \langle T \rangle_{ASW} \right) \tag{10.4.7}$$

where

$$\langle T \rangle_{AFW} = \min f_{AFW}, \quad f_{AFW} = a_1 K + \frac{a_2}{K} + a_3 \tag{10.4.8}$$

$$\left(K + V \right) \left(q_1 - q_3 \right) + q_2 \le 0 \tag{10.4.9}$$

and

$$\langle T \rangle_{ASW} = \min f_{ASW},$$

$$f_{ASW} = a_1 K + \frac{1}{K}\left[a_2 + q_4\left(q_2 + V\left(q_1 - q_3\right)\right)\right] \qquad (10.4.10)$$

$$+ a_3 - \left(K + V - q_4\right)\left(q_1 - q_3\right) - q_2,$$

$$\left(K + V\right)\left(q_1 - q_3\right) + q_2 > 0 \qquad (10.4.11)$$

as

$$0 < K \leq \langle M \rangle \qquad (10.4.12)$$

using the following notations:

$$a_1 = \sum_{j=1}^{J-1} \tau_{j,d}, \, a_2 = \langle M \rangle V\tau_{J,d}, \, a_3 = V\sum_{j=1}^{J-1} \tau_{j,d} + \left(\langle M \rangle + \frac{V}{2}\right)\tau_{J,d}$$

$$+ X\sum_{j=1}^{J} \tau_{j,u} + Y\sum_{j=1}^{J} \tau_{j,d} \qquad (10.4.13)$$

$$q_1 = \frac{1}{2}\sum_{j=1}^{J} \tau_{j,d}, \, q_2 = \frac{A}{2}\sum_{j=1}^{J} \tau_{j,u}, \, q_3 = \frac{N}{2}\tau_{1,d}, q_4 = \frac{2\langle M \rangle}{N}$$

The complete solution of system (Equation 10.4.7) to (Equation 10.4.12) is presented in Section 10.5.

10.5 Solution to the Problem and Decision Diagrams

Let us start with the case of $J > 1$, i.e., $a_1 > 0$. One has to consider three situations.

Case $q_1 > q_3$

First, consider Equation 10.4.8 and Equation 10.4.9. Inequality (Equation 10.4.9) can be presented as:

$$K \leq Q \qquad (10.5.1)$$

where the following notation is introduced:

$$Q \equiv -V - \frac{q_2}{q_1 - q_3} \qquad (10.5.2)$$

One can see that no positive solution K is possible here.

Now consider Equation 10.4.10 and Equation 10.4.11. Inequality (Equation 10.4.11) can be presented as:

$$K > Q \qquad (10.5.3)$$

There are two cases here to consider. At

$$a_1 - q_1 + q_3 > 0 \qquad (10.5.4)$$

as Q is negative (see Equation 10.5.2), one just has to minimize Equation 10.4.10 at positive K. This yields the following K value in the minimum point:

$$\sqrt{\frac{a_2 - q_4 Q(q_1 - q_3)}{a_1 - q_1 + q_3}} \qquad (10.5.5)$$

Combining Equation 10.5.5 with restriction (Equation 10.4.12) finally yields:

$$K_{opt} = \min\left(\sqrt{\frac{a_2 - q_4 Q(q_1 - q_3)}{a_1 - q_1 + q_3}}, \langle M \rangle\right) \qquad (10.5.6)$$

Solution (Equation 10.5.6) is illustrated in Figure 10.2.

At

$$a_1 - q_1 + q_3 \leq 0 \qquad (10.5.7)$$

the function minimized in Equation 10.4.10 monotonically decreases, and the solution is simply:

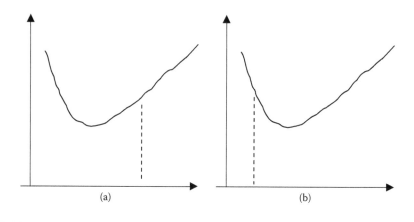

(a)   (b)

Figure 10.2   Graphical representation of the solution (Equation 10.5.6); (a) the minimum of the function in Equation 10.4.10 is on the left of $\langle M \rangle$ (shown by the dashed line); (b) the minimum of the function in Equation 10.4.10 is on the right of $\langle M \rangle$.

$$K_{opt} = \langle M \rangle \tag{10.5.8}$$

Case $q_1 < q_3$

First, consider Equation 10.4.8. and Equation 10.4.9. Inequality (Equation 10.4.9) can be presented as:

$$K \geq Q \tag{10.5.9}$$

The value of Q may be of both signs.
   At

$$Q > \langle M \rangle \tag{10.5.10}$$

no solution of Equation 10.4.8, Equation 10.4.9, and Equation 10.4.12 is possible.
   At

$$Q \leq \langle M \rangle \tag{10.5.11}$$

the solution is (see Figure 10.3):

$$K_{\text{opt}} = \max\left\{Q, \min\left\{\sqrt{\frac{a_2}{a_1}}, \langle M\rangle\right\}\right\} \tag{10.5.12}$$

Now, consider Equation 10.4.10 and Equation 10.4.11. Inequality (Equation 10.4.11) can be presented as:

$$K < Q \tag{10.5.13}$$

and the solution exists at $Q > 0$. Again, there are two cases to consider. At

$$a_1 - q_1 + q_3 > 0 \tag{10.5.14}$$

the solution is:

$$K_{\text{opt}} = \min\left\{\sqrt{\frac{a_2 - q_4 Q(q_1 - q_3)}{a_1 - q_1 + q_3}}, \min\left\{Q, \langle M\rangle\right\}\right\} \tag{10.5.15}$$

At

$$a_1 - q_1 + q_3 \le 0 \tag{10.5.16}$$

the function minimized in Equation 10.4.10 monotonically decreases (Figure10.4), and the solution is:

$$K_{\text{opt}} = \min\left\{Q, \langle M\rangle\right\} \tag{10.5.17}$$

Case $q_1 = q_3$

In this case, the solution is obtained simply from Equation 10.5.6:

$$K_{\text{opt}} = \min\left(\sqrt{\frac{a_2}{a_1}}, \langle M\rangle\right) \tag{10.5.18}$$

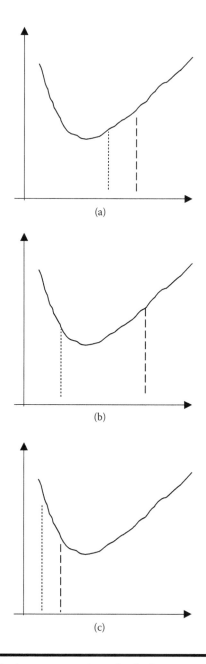

Figure 10.3 **Graphical representation of solution (Equation 10.5.12); (a) the minimum of the function in Equation 10.4.8 is on the left of both ⟨M⟩ (shown by the dashed line) and Q (shown by the dotted line); (b) the minimum of the function in Equation 10.4.8 is between ⟨M⟩ and Q; (c) the minimum of the function in Equation 10.4.8 is on the right of both ⟨M⟩ and Q.**

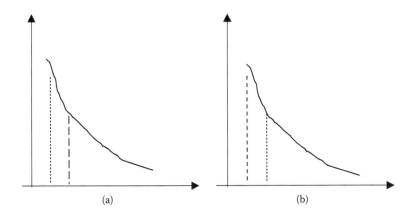

Figure 10.4 Graphical representation of solution (Equation 10.5.17). The function in Equation 10.4.10 monotonically decreases; ⟨M⟩ is shown by the dashed line and Q by the dotted line. (a) ⟨M⟩ on the right of Q; (b) ⟨M⟩ on the left of Q.

so one can just use Equation 10.5.6 that includes the solution (Equation 10.5.18).

The solution presented here at J > 1 yields the decision diagram shown in Figure 10.5. The decision diagram at J = 1 is obtained in the limit of $a_1 \rightarrow 0$ and is shown in Figure 10.6.

10.6 Extension of the Method in the Case of a Fixed MAC Frame Length

For a protocol with a fixed MAC frame length, the problem can be reduced to the one considered in this section.

When the MAC frames are required to be of the same length, message lengths are not necessarily an integer multiple of the packet length. The last packet of a TCP/IP message will have to contain extra bits, called the *fill* [1], to bring it up to the required length. The effect of the fill is an additional loss of performance, especially if the fixed packet length exceeds those of many TCP/IP messages.

The fill length F is determined as follows:

$$F = K - M + \left(\left\lceil \frac{M}{K} \right\rceil - 1 \right) \times K \qquad (10.6.1)$$

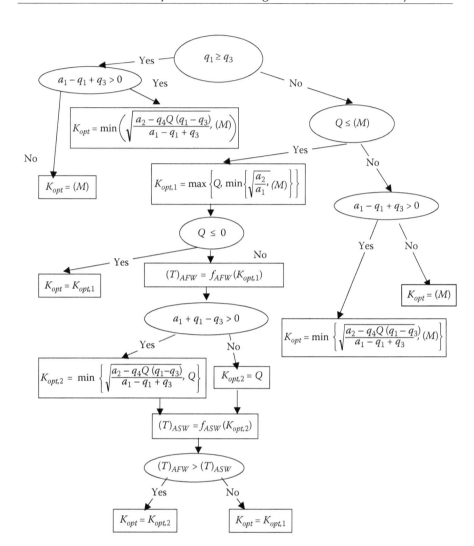

Figure 10.5   Decision diagram for determining the optimum MAC packet size at J > 1.

Introducing Equation 10.2.5 into Equation 10.6.1 yields:

$$F = \frac{K}{2} \tag{10.6.2}$$

Using Equation 10.6.2 yields the following expression for $\langle T \rangle$:

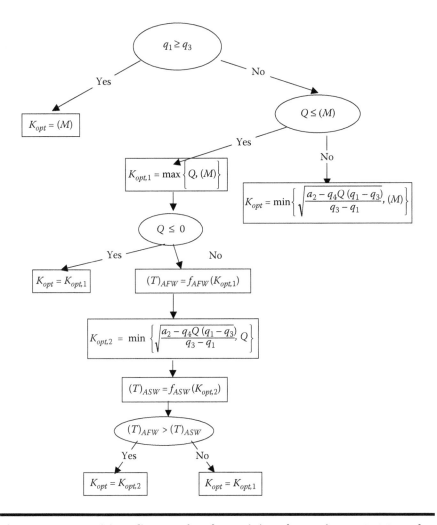

Figure 10.6 Decision diagram for determining the optimum MAC packet size at J = 1.

$$\langle T \rangle = (K + V) \sum_{j=1}^{J-1} \tau_{j,d} + \left(\langle M \rangle + \frac{\langle M \rangle}{K} V + \frac{V}{2} + \frac{K}{2} \right) \tau_{J,d}$$

$$+ \left(\frac{1}{N} \left(0.5 + \frac{\langle M \rangle}{K} \right) - 0.5 \right) E(K) \cdot h(E(K)) \qquad (10.6.3)$$

$$+ X \sum_{j=1}^{J} \tau_{j,u} + Y \sum_{j=1}^{J} \tau_{j,d}$$

One can see from Equation 10.6.3 that the whole analysis performed in the case of variable frame length can be repeated here, with a_1 in Equation 10.4.13 redefined as follows:

$$a_1 = \sum_{j=1}^{J-1} \tau_{j,d} + 0.5 \cdot \tau_{J,d} \qquad (10.6.4)$$

In this case, a_1 is always positive (even in the single-hop case) so that at both $J > 1$ and $J = 1$, one has the same decision diagram shown in Figure 10.5.

10.7 Extension of the Method to Account for Error Detection and Retransmission in the TCP/IP Protocol

The role of error control via retransmissions in the procedure of determining the optimal MAC packet size is discussed in this section. Specifically, the method developed in the preceding text will be extended to account for TCP/IP error control.

The error control in TCP/IP consists of including the cyclic redundancy check (CRC) field in each MAC packet at the source node. The value in this field is checked against the packet data on the destination node. If a mismatch occurs, a negative acknowledgment is sent back to the source node, causing packet retransmission. This is the essence of the selective automatic repeat request (ARQ) method in TCP/IP.

As long as one erroneous packet does not cause other packets to be retransmitted, the expected number of transmissions per successful transmission, ν, appears as a multiplicative factor in the TCP/IP message transaction time/throughput expressions; i.e., one has to use $\nu\langle T\rangle$ instead of $\langle T\rangle$ in the minimization criterion. The quantity ν can be expressed in the following form:

$$\nu = 1\cdot(1-P) + 2\cdot(1-P)P + \ldots + \chi\cdot(1-P)P^{\chi-1} + \chi\cdot P^{\chi} = \frac{1-P^{\chi}}{1-P} \qquad (10.7.1)$$

where χ is the maximum allowable number of transmissions per packet, and P is the packet error rate. Equation 10.7.1 means that a frame is either good at the first, second, or (χ – 1)th transmission, or it is erroneous at the χ-th transmission and is still accepted at the destination node. At large χ, Equation 10.7.1 reduces to:

$$v = \frac{1}{1 - P} \tag{10.7.2}$$

The packet error rate is [1]:

$$P = 1 - \left(1 - \varepsilon\right)^K \tag{10.7.3}$$

where ε is the bit error rate in the system. For a typical wireless link, P does not exceed 0.1 (Crow et al [5]); thus, the quantity $v = (1 - \varepsilon)^{-K}$ can be replaced by $(1 + K\varepsilon)$. To reflect this change in the decision diagram, one should determine K minimizing the functions:

$$\left(1 + K\varepsilon\right) f_{AFW}\left(K\right), \left(1 + K\varepsilon\right) f_{ASW}\left(K\right) \tag{10.7.4}$$

as power series with respect to ε. Applying standard perturbation methods yields:

$$K_{opt}\left(\varepsilon\right) = K_{opt}\left(0\right) - \varepsilon f\left(K\right)/f''\left(K\right)\big|_{K_{opt}(0)} + O\left(\varepsilon^2\right) \tag{10.7.5}$$

where f is either f_{AFW} or f_{ASW}, and $f'\left(K_{opt}(0)\right) = 0$. It follows from Equation 10.7.5, Equation 10.4.8, and Equation 10.4.10 that accounting for error control lowers K_{opt}.

10.8 Application to 802.11-Compliant Networks

Generally, each particular case should be analyzed using decision diagrams obtained previously. In this section, we will discuss a limiting case of large N, which corresponds to the AFW scenario. In the case of variable MAC frame length, let us consider a network with homogeneous parameters, neglecting transmission errors. The coefficients defined in Equation 10.4.13 simplify as follows:

$$a_1 = \left(J - 1\right)\tau, a_2 = \left\langle M\right\rangle V\tau, a_3 = V\left(J - 1\right)\tau + \left(\left\langle M\right\rangle + \frac{V}{2}\right)\tau + \left(X + Y\right)J\tau$$

$$q_1 = \frac{J\tau}{2}, q_2 = \frac{AJ\tau}{2}, q_3 = \frac{N}{2}\tau, q_4 = \frac{2\left\langle M\right\rangle}{N}$$

Therefore, at J > 1, the optimal MAC packet size is:

$$K_{opt} = \sqrt{\frac{a_2}{a_1}} = \sqrt{\frac{\langle M \rangle V}{J-1}} \qquad (10.8.1)$$

and it is equal to $\langle M \rangle$ at J = 1. The TCP/IP message transaction time is:

$$\frac{\langle T \rangle}{\tau} = (K+V)(J-1) + \langle M \rangle + \frac{\langle M \rangle}{K}V + \frac{V}{2} + (X+Y)J \qquad (10.8.2)$$

Combining Equation 10.2.10 and Equation 10.8.2 yields the ratio R/R_{max}:

$$\frac{R}{R_{max}} = \frac{(K_{opt}+V)(J-1) + \langle M \rangle + \dfrac{\langle M \rangle}{K_{opt}}V + \dfrac{V}{2} + (X+Y)J}{(K+V)(J-1) + \langle M \rangle + \dfrac{\langle M \rangle}{K}V + \dfrac{V}{2} + (X+Y)J} \qquad (10.8.3)$$

where K_{opt} is given by Equation 10.8.1 at J > 1 and $K_{opt} = K_{max}$ (maximum size of the MAC packet allowed by the communication protocol) at J = 1.

Equation 10.8.3 was used to estimate the effect of the MAC packet size on the throughput. Typical data for networks compliant with the 802.11 wireless LAN standard were used [2]. Specifically, V = 34 bytes and X = Y = 16 bytes; K_{max} = 2300 bytes for $\langle M \rangle$ exceeding 2300 bytes, and it is equal to $\langle M \rangle$ for $\langle M \rangle$ smaller than 2300 bytes.

Figure 10.7 shows dependencies of the relative throughput on K for different numbers of links J in the network path at $\langle M \rangle$ = 2300 bytes. As expected, for the one-link path, the throughput increases as K increases. Multihop paths shown are characterized by the throughput curves with a maximum at K_{opt} = 280, 198, and 161, for J = 2, 3, and 4, respectively. At K = 2300 (i.e., if the source node chooses the maximum allowed packet size instead of the optimal one), the throughput is about 0.63, 0.46, and 0.37 of the maximum values, for J = 2, 3, and 4, respectively.

Effects of the total number of links, J, in the wireless path are further illustrated in Table 10.1. One can see that the optimum packet size decreases as J increases. Using the optimum packet size instead of the maximum allowable packet size becomes increasingly beneficial

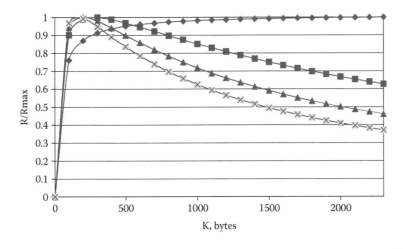

Figure 10.7 **Relative throughput for a multihop network path as a function of the MAC packet size. Diamonds, squares, triangles, and stars label curves for J = 1, 2, 3, and 4, respectively.**

Table 10.1 **Optimal MAC Packet Size and Related Throughput Characteristics versus the Number of Links in a Network Path**

J	K_{opt}, Bytes	$R(K_{max})/R(K_{opt})$	$(R(K_{opt}) - R(K_{max}))/R(K_{max})$, %
1	2000	1	0
2	280	0.63	60
3	198	0.46	117
4	161	0.37	170
5	140	0.31	217

as J increases. But even in the case of a two-link path, an increase in throughput owing to using the optimum size instead of the maximum one is as large as 60 percent.

Effects of the average TCP/IP message length, $\langle M \rangle$, on the throughput are further illustrated in Table 10.2. A two-hop path was considered. One can see that the optimum packet size increases as M increases. Using the optimum packet size instead of the maximum allowable packet size becomes less effective as M increases.

Tables 10.2   Optimal MAC Packet Size and Related Throughput Characteristics versus the TCP/IP Message Size

$\langle M \rangle$	K_{opt}, Bytes	$R(K_{max})/R(K_{opt})$	$(R(K_{opt})R(K_{max}))/R(K_{max})$, %
2000	280	0.63	60
4000	369	0.75	33
8000	522	0.87	15
16000	738	0.94	6

Finally, consider the effect of X and Y on the results. It can be seen from equations presented in the preceding text that the optimum MAC frame size is independent of X and Y. But the throughput does depend on these parameters, and it decreases for larger X or Y values.

What was presented in this section is a simplified numerical analysis, as the window flow control and heterogeneity of transport parameters were not considered. However, it clearly shows possible performance benefits of properly selecting K_{opt} in CTRF networks.

10.9 Conclusions

Bertsekas and Gallager in their work [1] considered a simpler version of the MAC packet size optimization problem in a TCP/IP session. Compared to [1], the problem considered in this chapter accounts for the transmission delay of acknowledgment frames, the sliding window flow control in TCP/IP protocol, heterogeneity of transport parameters (link-to-link and upstream/downstream) along a multihop network path, and the error control via retransmissions. In this chapter, possible practical applications of the method are discussed.

Decision diagrams developed in this chapter can be useful in real CTRF networks such as wireless LANs, as well as in networks consisting of both CTRF and CTR components (such as IEEE-802.3-compliant networks). In the latter case, each continuous part belonging to a CTR network should be treated as a single link of the network path considered. Determining delays τ_j on each link can be performed upon requests from the source node sent over the network path. The TCP/IP protocol suite includes the Internet Control Messaging Protocol (ICMP) that helps identify network problems such as incorrect gateway settings, unavailable applications or processes, and fragmentation problems (Stevens [6]). An application of ICMP relevant to our discussion is sending and receiving time stamp requests and replies. For instance, the *tracert* utility in UNIX uses these ICMP messages for measuring delays on the links of a network path. Similarly, the source node can use these ICMP features for collecting τ_j statistics, computing the coefficients in Equation 10.4.13, and then precalculating the optimal MAC packet size using the decision diagrams in Figure 10.5 and Figure 10.6. The advantage of this approach to throughput optimization is that it requires modification of TCP/IP code only on the source node of the path, whereas the destination node just complies with the K_{opt} value proposed upstream.

In 802.11 networks, there is another, intrinsic option for collecting τ_j statistics, e.g., via a virtual carrier sense (CS) mechanism implemented in the media access layer. This mechanism is discussed by Xu and Saadawi in Reference 7, in which they performed simulations and throughput analysis for 802.11 multihop networks. Specifically, to reduce the probability of two stations colliding owing to not hearing each other, the virtual CS mechanism works as follows. A station wanting to transmit a packet first transmits a short control packet called *request to send* (RTS) that includes the source, destination, and duration of the intended packet and acknowledgment transaction. If the medium is free, the destination station responds with a control packet called clear to send (CTS) that includes the same duration information. All other stations receiving RTS/CTS packets use this information together with the physical CS when sensing the medium. As this mechanism for collecting τ_j statistics does not require any special TCP/IP services, it appears more preferable in 802.11 networks than the ICMP mechanism.

Because breaking a TCP/IP message into MAC packets at the source node is always possible, not all TCP implementations use this option. However, packets are commonly fragmented, as they travel between the source and destination. Although reassembling the fragments at subsequent nodes is an option, it is typically not done. Therefore, our method can also be used for an optimal fragmentation of a MAC packet traveling between an intermediate node (deciding to fragment it) and the destination node of a network path.

To summarize, in this chapter we presented a new analytical method for optimally breaking a TCP/IP message into MAC packets in networks without cut-through routing (such as networks compliant with the IEEE 802.11 and IEEE 802.16 wireless standards). Compared to the earlier work of Bertsekas and Gallager [1], our method also accounts for the transmission delay of acknowledgment frames, the sliding window flow control in TCP/IP protocol, error control via selective ARQ, and heterogeneity of transport parameters (link-to-link and upstream/downstream) along a multihop network path. Mathematically, the problem consists of minimizing the TCP/IP message transaction time, a nonlinear function of the MAC packet size, in the presence of a set of linear restrictions. The problem has an exact solution presented in the form of a decision diagram. In the limit of large sliding window size, the solution further simplifies and is applied to the throughput analysis using IEEE 802.11 data. Possible applications of the method for optimization in pure CTRF networks, as well as more complex CTRF and CTR combinations, will require collecting statistics on delays, either in the TCP/IP layer (ICMP messages) or in the media access layer (e.g., for IEEE 802.11 networks, using the virtual CS mechanism).

References

1. Bertsekas, D., Gallager, R., *Data Networks,* Upper Saddle River, NJ: Prentice Hall, 1992.
2. IEEE 802.11: *Wireless LAN Medium Access Control (MAC) and Physical Layer (PHY) Specifications,* IEEE, 1999.
3. IEEE 802.16: *Preliminary Draft Working Document for 802.16 Broadband Wireless Access System Requirements,* IEEE 802.16s0-99/5, Oct. 1999.
4. Kleinrock, L., *Communication Nets: Stochastic Message Flow and Delay,* New York: McGraw-Hill, 1964.
5. Crow, B.P., Widjaja, I., Geun Kim, J., and Sakai, P.T., IEEE 802.11 wireless local area networks, *IEEE Commun. Mag.*, Vol. 35(9), 116–126, September 1997.
6. Richard Stevens, W., *TCP/IP Illustrated, Volume 1: The Protocols,* New York: Addison-Wesley, 1994.
7. Xu, S., Saadawi, T., Does the IEEE 802.11 MAC protocol work well in multihop wireless ad hoc networks?, *IEEE Commun. Mag.*, Vol. 39(6), 130–137, June 2001.
8. Mitlin, V., Optimal MAC packet size in networks without cut-through routing, *IEEE Trans. Wireless Commun.*, Vol. 2, 901–910, 2003.
9. Mitlin, V., Corrections to optimal MAC packet size in networks without cut-through routing, *IEEE Trans. Wireless Commun.*, Vol. 2, p. 1275, 2003.

Appendix A

Optimization Puzzles

In this section, I have collected some optimization puzzles for the reader's amusement. Do not get frustrated if you cannot solve them right away; some of these puzzles just take some time to crack. Good luck.

A.1

There are 12 coins. One of them is counterfeit; it weighs differently. It is not known if the false coin is heavier or lighter than the right coins. How would you find the false coin with no more than three weighs on a simple scale?

A.2

A group of four people have to cross a bridge. It is dark, and they have to light the path with a flashlight. No more than two people can cross the bridge simultaneously, and the group has only one flashlight. Each individual takes a different amount of time to cross the bridge: Annie crosses the bridge in 1 min, Bob crosses the bridge in 2 min, Carole crosses the bridge in 5 min, and Dorothy crosses the bridge in 10 min. How can the group cross the bridge in 17 min?

A.3

The distance between the towns A and B is 1000 mi. There are 3000 apples in A, and these have to be delivered to B. The available car can take 1000 apples at the most. The driver has an apple addiction — when he has apples on board, he eats one apple for every mile he drives. Figure out the strategy that yields the largest amount of apples to be delivered to B.

A.4

A Buddhist monk receives a task from his teacher — to meditate for exactly 45 min. He has no watch; instead, he is given two sticks of incense, and he is told that each of the sticks would completely burn in 1 hr. The sticks are not identical, and they burn with variable yet unknown rates (they are handmade). Thus, with these two incense sticks and some matches, can he arrange for exactly 45 min of meditation?

A.5

A galaxy consists of three planets, each of them moving along a straight line at its own constant speed. If the centers of all three planets happen to lie on a straight line (some kind of eclipse), the inhabitants of each planet go nuts (they cannot see their two neighbor planets all at once); they start talking about the end of the world, and the stock markets crash. Show that there will be no more than two such market crashes on each of these planets.

A.6

Dragon brainstorm in a convention center: Delegates have to be selected so as to provide maximum efficiency. A dragon can have any number of heads. For any N, any number of N-headed dragons are available as needed. The problem is that the size of the convention center is limited such that no more than 1000 heads can fit into the assembly hall. The intellectual power of a dragon pack is the product of head numbers of the dragons in the pack. What is the optimum pack population (the total number of dragons and the head number distribution)?

A.7

On the surface of a planet lives a vampire that can move with a speed not greater than u. A vampire slayer spaceship travels at the speed v. As soon as the spaceship sees a vampire, it shoots a silver bullet, and the vampire is killed. Prove that if v/u > 10, the vampire slayer can accomplish this mission, even if the vampire is trying to hide.

A.8

Two-dimensional case: A projector illuminates a quadrant on a plane. Four projectors are set in four arbitrary points of the plane. Show that they can be turned such that the whole plane would be illuminated. Three-dimensional case: Show that the whole space can be illuminated with eight projectors, each illuminating an octant, wherever the location points are.

A.9

Salt Lake City looks like a rectangle crossed, with **M** streets going from North to South and **N** streets going from East to West. The city is frequently visited by tourists who are supposed to travel in buses. The Utah governor wants to monitor all movement of the buses. He plans to put policemen at some intersections to watch all the buses moving on the streets visible from these intersections. What is the minimum number of policemen needed?

A.10

Consider a rectangular M × N checkerboard with some checkers on it. What is the minimum number of checkers you should put on the board such that any straight line parallel to any one of two sides of the board would cross some (at least one) checker?

A.11

A group of soldiers expects a captain's visit. There are two rows of soldiers, one behind the other, and any soldier in the second row is taller than the soldier in front of him. The captain shows up, sees the picture, and commands the soldiers in each row to rearrange themselves according to their heights. Prove that in the final arrangement any soldier in the second row will still be taller than the soldier in front of him.

A.12

A larger group of soldiers expects a general's visit. They are arranged in a rectangle such that a soldier in each column is taller than the soldier in front of him. The general shows up, sees the picture, and commands the soldiers in each row to rearrange themselves according to their heights. Prove that in the final arrangement any soldier in each column will still be taller than the soldier in front of him.

A.13

Ivan Susanin rehearses his famous act. A typical training exercise consists of the following: He starts somewhere inside a circular forest preserve. He has a map and a compass. He goes straight, turns left, goes straight, turns left, goes straight again, then turns left, and so on until he returns to the initial point. There, he says, "Oops!", waves his hat, cries out "*Zhizn' za tsarya!*" ("Life for the Czar!"), and falls on the ground. The circular forest preserve has a radius of 1 km. Susanin's route is a polygon with N sides, and he has to stay in the forest all the time during the exercise. Now, though he can observe the right angles in his turns (he has a compass), he sometimes misses the turn points. As a result, he will not return to the initial point, will not say "Oops!", will not wave his hat, will not cry out "Zhizn' za tsarya!", and will not fall on the ground. It is known that the relative error in Susanin's estimate of the length of each side of the polygon does not exceed P. Let the distance between the point to which he returns and the one to which he was supposed to return, be equal to D. Show that $D < (N - 1)*P$.

A.14

There are N leaves on the ground, and every two of them overlap somewhere. A caterpillar moves along a straight line and eats whatever is in its way. Show that it can choose a path to be able to taste all leaves.

A.15

There are two jars, with M marbles in the first jar and N marbles in the second (M > N). Two kids play the following game: one of them takes from a jar a number of marbles proportional to the total number of marbles in the other jar. Next, the other kid does the same until somebody (the winner) takes the last marble from a jar. At what ratios q = M/N will the first kid have a winning strategy?

A.16

There are two people: one has a diamond, a suitcase, a padlock, and a key to the padlock; the other has another padlock and a key to this lock. The diamond has to be sent by mail from the first person to the other. Everything sent in the mail and not locked inside the suitcase will be stolen. Can the diamond be safely transported?

A.17

One has to break a chocolate bar into pieces. This is a rectangular bar consisting of M x N pieces. One can break the bar only along the dividing lines, and one may not stack the pieces when breaking them. What is the strategy yielding the minimum number of operations to separate out all the elementary pieces?

Matlab Scripts for the Bandwidth Optimization Problem

B.1

This Matlab script was developed to provide a numerical proof of the fact that the phi-pulse is bandwidth-optimal among all pulses generated by SAS containing three adders.

```
ind=0;
for pp=2:256
    rr=11111111111111111111111111;
    p=pp-1;
    x=zeros(p);
    for i =1:p
        np=p-i+1;
        for j=1:np
            m=np-j+1;
             a=boxcar(i);
            b=boxcar(j);
            c=boxcar(m);
            x=conv(conv(a,b),c);
```

```
            g=0;f=0;h=0;
            for k=2:p
                    g=g+(x(k)-x(k-1))^2;
                    h=h+(x(k)*x(k));
            end
            g=g+(x(p))^2+(x(1))^2;
            h=h+(x(1)*x(1));
            r=g-f*f/(pp);r=r/h;
            if(rr>r)
                    xr=x;
                    ir=i;
                    jr=j;
                    mr=m;
                    rr=r;
            end
        end
end
exact=round(3*pp/8);
if(floor(0.375*pp)+0.5==(0.375*pp))
    exact=floor(0.375*pp);
end
if (jr==exact)
    ind=ind+1;
end
pp
exact
itisnophi=ind-p
% end of script
```

B.2

This Matlab script was developed to provide a numerical proof of the fact that the phi-pulse is bandwidth-optimal among all pulses generated by SAS containing four adders.

```
ind=0;
for pp=2:36
    rr=11111111111111111111111;
    p=pp-1;
    x=zeros(p);
    for i =1:ceil(p/2+1)
```

```
        np=p-i+1;
        for j=1:np
                m=np-j+1;
                for j1=1:m
                        m1=m-j1+1;
                        a=boxcar(i);
                        b=boxcar(j);
                        c=boxcar(j1);
                        d=boxcar(m1);
                        x=conv(conv(conv(a,b),c),d);
                        g=0;f=0;h=0;
                        for k=2:p
                                g=g+(x(k)-x(k-1))^2;
                                f=f+(x(k)-x(k-1));
                                h=h+(x(k)*x(k));
                        end
                        g=g+(x(p))^2+(x(1))^2;
                        f=f-(x(p))+(x(1));
                        h=h+(x(1)*x(1));
                        r=g-f*f/(pp+1);r=r/h;
                        if(rr>r)
                                xr=x;
                                ir=i;
                                jr=j;
                                mr=j1;
                                m1r=m1;
                                rr=r;
                        end
                end
        end
end
exact=round(3*pp/8);
if(floor(0.375*pp)+0.5==(0.375*pp))
        exact=floor(0.375*pp);
end
if (mr==exact)
        ind=ind+1;
end
pp
exact
itisnophi=ind-p
% end of script
```

B.3

This Matlab script was developed to find the pulse providing the minimum to the spectral width, as described in Chapter 4.

```
ind=0;
pp=32;rr=777777777777777777;
pp1=round(pp*20);p=pp-1;crit=96/(9*pp*pp+16);
x=zeros(p);
iin=zeros(2,1);
xrr=zeros(p);
xrrr=zeros(p);
for i =1:p
    iin=randint(2,1,2);
    x(i)=pp1+sin(i);
end
while(ind<10000)
    hj=ceil(ind/1000)/1;
    iin=randint(2,1,p);
    i=iin(1,1)+1;
    j=iin(2,1)+1;
    x(i)=x(i)+hj;
    x(j)=x(j)-hj;
    g=0;f=0;h=0;
    for k=2:p
        g=g+(x(k)-x(k-1))^2;
        f=f+(x(k)-x(k-1));
        h=h+(x(k)*x(k));
    end
    g=g+(x(p))^2+(x(1))^2;
    f=f-(x(p))+(x(1));
    h=h+(x(1)*x(1));
    r=g-f*f/(pp);r=r/h/h/h;
    if(rr>r)
        rr=r
        ind=0;
    else
        x(i)=x(i)-hj;
        ind=ind+1;
        x(j)=x(j)+hj;
    end
end
dt=1/pp;im=pp/2;
```

```
xmax=x(im);
for i=1:p
    u=i*dt;
    xrr(i)=(4*u*(1-u))^2;
    x(i)=x(i)/xmax;
end
k=1:1:p;xrr=sin(pi*k/pp);
g=0;f=0;h=0;
for k=2:p
    g=g+(xrr(k)-xrr(k-1))^2;
    f=f+(xrr(k)-xrr(k-1));
    h=h+(xrr(k)*xrr(k));
end
g=g+(xrr(p))^2+(xrr(1))^2;
f=f-(xrr(p))+(xrr(1));
h=h+(xrr(1)*xrr(1));
rrrr=g-f*f/(pp);rrrr=rrrr/h;
critb=12/(pp*pp+2);
exact=round(3*pp/8);
if(floor(0.375*pp)+0.5==(0.375*pp))
    exact=floor(0.375*pp);
end
a=boxcar(exact);
b=boxcar(p-exact+1);
xrrr=conv(a,b);
for i =1:p
    xrrr(i)=xrrr(i)/exact;
end
g=0;f=0;h=0;
for k=2:p
    g=g+(xrrr(k)-xrrr(k-1))^2;
    f=f+(xrrr(k)-xrrr(k-1));
    h=h+(xrrr(k)*xrrr(k));
end
g=g+(xrrr(p))^2+(xrrr(1))^2;
f=f-(xrrr(p))+(xrrr(1));
h=h+(xrrr(1)*xrrr(1));
rrrrr=g-f*f/(pp);rrrrr=rrrrr/h;
ss=1:p
figure(1);
plot(ss,x,'-',ss,xrr,':',ss,xrrr,'--')
% end of script
```

Appendix C

More about Flat Spectrum Chirps

Let us define the q-point DFT of a sequence **z** as follows:

$$\text{DFT}(\vec{z}) = \frac{1}{q^{1/2}} \sum_{k=0}^{q-1} z_k \exp(-2\pi j k n / q) \qquad (\text{C}.1)$$

FSC is a complex sequence of a unit envelope with DFT of a unit envelope.

We found that FSCs have another remarkable property, e.g., applying to an FSC the DFT twice yields the same FSC. The proof is numerical. Specifically, a Matlab script was written that, for given q and p, it computes several functions of p and q. The first function is:

$$r(q,p) = 1 - \text{sign}\left[\left(\gcd(q,p) + (q\%2) \cdot (p\%2) - 1\right)^2\right] \qquad (\text{C}.2)$$

In Equation (C.2), gcd stands for the greatest common divisor of two natural numbers, and % denotes computing a remainder of division one integer by another. The function r equals 1 for mutually prime p and q of opposite parity, and it equals 0 otherwise. The second function is:

$$d(q,p) = 1 - \text{sign}\left[\left|\vec{z}(q,p) - \text{DFT}\left(\text{DFT}\left(\vec{z}(q,p)\right)\right)\right|^2\right] \quad \text{(C.3)}$$

In Equation (C.3), the vector **z** corresponds to a sequence defined by Equation (5.3.1).

The function d equals 1 if the double DFT of **z** coincides with **z**, and it equals 0 otherwise. The third and the fourth functions are:

$$R(M,Q) = \sum_{q=M}^{Q}\sum_{p=1}^{q} r(q,p) \qquad D(M,Q) = \sum_{q=M}^{Q}\sum_{p=1}^{q} d(q,p) \quad \text{(C.4)}$$

In Equations (C.4), M and Q are positive integers, M<Q.

We computed the dependence R(D) at M=2 and Q running between 2 and 256. We found that the R=D for all Q from this interval, which constitutes the numerical proof of the statement made in the beginning of Appendix C. It follows from this result that a sequence **Z**=DFT(FSC) is a complex, unit-envelope sequence mapped by the DFT to another complex, unit-envelope sequence. **Z** is termed the dual FSC (DFSC).

The result we just proved means that one can write:

$$\text{DFT}\left[\vec{z} + \text{DFT}(\vec{z})\right] = \text{DFT}\left(\vec{z}\right) + \text{DFT}\left(\text{DFT}\left(\vec{z}\right)\right) = \text{DFT}\left(\vec{z}\right) + \vec{z} \quad \text{(C.5)}$$

e.g., the sum of an FSC and its corresponding DFSC is equal to its DFT. We termed this sum the "basic spectrum-shaped waveform" (BSSW).

As the DFT is a linear operation, any linear combination of several BSSWs will be a spectrum-shaped waveform. We termed them "derivative spectrum-shaped waveforms." For a given q, there is an innumerous amount of different DSSWs.

Index

Milton Keynes UK
Ingram Content Group UK Ltd.
UKHW040059071024
449327UK00019B/674